Hey, good lookin'—what ya got cookin'?

This is what Dolly Parton sings to her sister Rachel Parton George whenever she walks into her kitchen. It's what you do when a love for good music and good food runs in the family.

In *Good Lookin' Cookin'* Dolly and Rachel share tips for hosting events all year long, including twelve multicourse menus of cherished recipes for New Year's Day, Easter, Mother's Day, Thanksgiving, Christmas, and more. You'll learn how much butter or whipped cream goes into a "Dolly Dollop," what condiment is almost always on the table at Parton family meals, and what special dish Rachel makes at Dolly's request every year for her birthday. Recipes include American classics such as Country Ham and Biscuits, Barbecue Ribs, Family Favorite Meatloaf, Slaw of Many Colors, Watermelon Fruit Salad, Mac and Cheese, and Strawberry Shortcake.

Filled with more than 80 delicious dishes as well as photographs of Dolly and Rachel cooking and hosting all year long, *Good Lookin' Cookin'* is a treasured cookbook that will make you feel like part of the Parton family. With their trademark warmth and sisterly love, Dolly and Rachel remind you that cooking doesn't need to be serious—it should be fun! And always good lookin'!

Good Lookin' Cookin'

CLUB

Good Lookin' Cookin'

A YEAR OF MEALS: A LIFETIME OF FAMILY, FRIENDS, AND FOOD

Dolly Parton
&
Rachel Parton George

with Maurice Miner

Photographs by Aubrie Pick

TEN SPEED PRESS
California | New York

We dedicate this book to every person who has ever raided a garden, opened a refrigerator, held a spatula, or put a skillet or a pot on the stove to furnish love and nourishment to those they hold dear, and to those who believe that good food and good times are the next best thing to pure love. We also dedicate this book to all the friends and family who have contributed to and helped in any way to make this something we both are very proud of. Enjoy!

— Dolly & Rachel

Contents

Recipes

July

August

September

October

November

December

A Message from Dolly

God, family, music, and food are the staples of my life. Food for the heart, food for the mind, food for the soul, and food for the table. Rachel and I come from a long line of great cooks—our mama, our grandmothers, our aunts, cousins, and so on.

"Hey, good lookin'—what ya got cookin'?" It's a phrase from the old Hank Williams song we've used forever when we walk into someone's kitchen. Sometimes we say it; sometimes we sing it. It fits here, though, and for several reasons.

A lot of my relatives are beautiful women—a lot of those same women are part of that long line of great cooks—so that seemed like a perfect title for our cookbook. And hey—Rachel's one of them. She is beautiful on the inside and out.

Rachel is Mama and Daddy's last child, but I've always claimed her as my own. She's a wonderful singer and songwriter, and she spent time out there on the road with me for many years in our traveling family band. She also acted in the TV series *9 to 5*. When it ended, though, she said, "Enough of this. I want to stay closer to home, raise a family, and cook," and she did.

What people may not know is that Rachel is the executive director of my company and pretty much runs my life. And thank goodness she does! But I think cooking is at the very top of her list of things she does best. I feel like I am kind of riding in on her coattails (or dress tail) on this one, but I am proud that we have something wonderful to do together that will last forever and hopefully bring as much joy and nourishment to others through the years as it has to us. Even though I am a very good cook, my dishes are not always as good lookin' as Rachel's. She has a true knack for making food look and taste beautiful, and that is truly an art.

We have had a wonderful time putting this together. And though it's a lot of work to do a project like this, we will always remember the time we spent together, creating this for you. Enjoy!

Dolly

A Message from Rachel

I am a collector—a collector of recipes and cookbooks. It's my hobby and my passion. There is only one thing I enjoy more than reading a good cookbook, and that's cooking a great meal for people to enjoy. No matter how far we travel—the places we visit, the food that we get to experience—there's nothing like home cookin'. And that's made even better when the time spent in the kitchen finds me joined by those I love. I've been blessed with family and friends who enjoy sharing recipes, not to mention new ideas for how to approach an old recipe. Sometimes they add a little something, swap out an ingredient, or choose to let things simmer a bit longer. I've tried virtually all of them! I love each and every recipe and each and every person who shared all of them with me.

It seems like everyone has that one dish, that one smell from the kitchen that takes them back home. I do. And I'm thrilled to share many of them here.

I have been cooking most of my life. At the age of five, our mama taught me how to make cornbread, and I've never stopped. I wish I'd written down her recipes as she cooked. She knew how to make anything, even with modest ingredients. We would ask, "Mama, how did you make this taste so good?" She would always smile and say, "I made it with love."

Our mama kept all of us happy with her cooking, and that extended to cousins, friends, and neighbors. When we were growing up, everyone knew that Mama always had food cooking, and there was always enough. She would make a few more biscuits, a few more dumplings, a little more gravy, and make sure everyone was taken care of. And *welcome*. No one walked away from her table hungry.

Daddy did his part, too, raising hogs for meat and cows for milk that could also be made into butter. We grew a garden, canned the vegetables it gave us, and put food away for the winter. We had apple, pear, and peach trees; their fruit was turned into jellies and jams. There were berries of all sorts, too—the perfect filling for cobblers. We even had walnut trees.

I've found in life there is nothing funnier than the truth, or more humbling. And the truth is we were poor. But we worked hard. One of my favorite jokes that Dolly loves to tell is how she responds when someone asks if we had running water—"Yes, when we'd run to get it!" It's true. Though Daddy grew tobacco as our money crop, we didn't have much.

But we did have each other. We had God and hope for a better tomorrow. We also had music. And we had Dolly. My sister is giving of her time, herself, her home. She made it out of poverty, and she took us with her. If she made a dime, she sent home a nickel. Whatever she has, she is more than willing to share—and does. It's a wonderful quality. To this day she is the most generous person that I know. Maybe that's why

God graced her with so much talent. I've heard her say a million times, "You can't outgive God!" Her heart is true, it's pure, and it's good. We truly are best friends.

I thank God every day for my family. We have such a good time together. We laugh, we cry, we talk, we say a few cuss words every now and again. And without fail—year after year—we gather together, often around a table, and celebrate all of that. Some of these recipes are longtime family favorites; some are our versions of dishes we've enjoyed over the years and learned to make ourselves. Many remind us of special people in our lives—I hope you enjoy getting to know us and our family through these meals.

So much of what you're about to enjoy and read is a credit, in part, to my mom, dad, brothers and sisters, aunts and uncles, cousins, friends, coworkers, neighbors, the internet, newspapers, magazines, and TV shows whose recipes have found their way into my collection. If you have given me a recipe over the years and I have added a little more of this or taken out a little bit of that, I hope you enjoy it . . . and I thank you.

In my home, food is a big part of how we connect and celebrate. I believe gathering for a meal feeds more than the body—it feeds the soul. I hope these recipes Dolly and I have collected to share will do the same for you.

Why We Love Cookin'

People often ask us, "Why do you love to cook?" "Because we love to eat!" we reply. That is the honest truth and the main reason for this book. But we're also creative people who like to make food that tastes great and looks beautiful. So, here we are with *Good Lookin' Cookin'*. The title may be inspired by a song lyric, but for us it's so much more.

It's meals we've made. It's recipes that are a reflection of who we are, where we come from, and the people who have been part of our lives. It's a year of meals—a menu that has meaning for each month, comprised of recipes we grew up with, recipes we discovered in our adult lives and travels, recipes that were shared with us by friends or family, and even some we created on our own. Now that we see them together—in this book you hold in your hands—we also realize this is more than a year of meals. It's a lifetime of family and friends and food.

Cooking and food have been part of our lives for as long as we can remember. Rachel has been cooking ever since the day Mama first let her help make cornbread at the age of five and Daddy told her at supper that night it was the best he'd ever tasted. Dolly stepped up and did a lot of the cooking back home, along with our sisters Willadeene, Stella, and Cassie, on those occasions when Mama wasn't well or was busy with everything else that accompanied having a dozen children. We spent a lot of time in the kitchen.

The kitchen—any kitchen—is so much more than a room. It's often the center of the home, and we all have memories of our mothers, grandmothers, and other wonderful women who have made us feel warm, fed, and safe there. From dawn to dusk, every piece of daily life that unfolded there contributed to our love of cooking. And that's because that room was filled with much more than warmth from the stovetop or oven—it was filled with the love of family.

Perhaps that's where the term "comfort food" comes from. And we believe there's something about food that *is* comforting. It brings people together. Preparing food allows you to express yourself. It's almost like a gift you've prepared with your hands to share with the people you love. Even the simplest dish can bring joy—to the person at the table who ultimately enjoys it and to the person who made it. We believe that—we know that—and it's why we love to cook.

Good food is good food. It doesn't have to be fancy, but it can be. It doesn't have to be simple, but it can be. There can be as much enjoyment in the finished result—the taste, seeing people gathered around the table—as there is in making it. This book, these meals, and our recipes are here in the hope that you'll do that. We want you to look at the food you make and say, "I can't wait to taste that!" We want you to enjoy the entire process, whether you're new to cooking or not, experienced or not, living on a budget or not, used to entertaining or not. Much of what you'll see on these pages is here because we decided to take a chance and try making it. And you know what? You can, too.

Don't get us wrong—we're not perfect cooks. We learned along the way, too, and not just from Mama. There may still be some spaghetti stuck to the ceiling and a spot or two of red sauce on the walls of Dolly and Carl's first home . . . and one Thanksgiving Rachel had to do some fast thinking when things didn't play out exactly as planned (just know that no one's ever going to complain about having extra gravy). But moments like those—which still provide joy as we laugh about them years later, even if we didn't in the moment—are more than offset by the number of unexpected, picture-perfect, "Wow! Look what I did!" moments, like the crème brûlée recipe in this book. Rachel just went for it, and it was beautiful. Like we've found is true of so many things in life, if you never try, you'll never know if you can, right? And that can be the case with food and in the kitchen. We've both had many moments where we've realized, "*Everyone* can do this. *Anyone* can do this."

And the truth is you can! Recipes should be easy—even if what ends up on the table looks like it wasn't. We're not complicated people. And who needs anything complicated in their life these days? Every recipe and every meal have a purpose, but you may be surprised to find out how much you can do with what you already have on hand. It helps to have an organized pantry that's stocked with the basics. The same holds true for your freezer. We can't tell you how many times we've thought, "There's nothing in this kitchen to make a meal." But just like Mama—who would grab something here and something there and before you knew it, there'd be a full meal on the table—we've discovered it's completely possible to create something from what seems like nothing. When we were first starting out, we each had about five recipes we could always bring out—two or three desserts, too. Having a few go-to's—and there are plenty in this book—will take you far.

It'll also allow you to enjoy the meal yourself. Everything we're sharing in these pages is meant to ensure that the person making these dishes gets to be at the table, spending time with their guests. Timing can be important. But a little simple planning—and we've tried to offer some ideas to help with that—will put you in your chair at the table along with everyone else as they enjoy the food you've prepared. And that's important.

It's often said that food can be comforting, but we feel it can be healing, too—healing to the mind, body, and soul. Dolly can do that with music; Rachel finds ways to do it with food. Together we've discovered we can even keep people near us in our memories because we're honoring them through food that they loved or shared with us.

The taste of a certain food, or the scent of it from the kitchen, can take you back so easily. Though we already knew that, we found it happening again and again as we put this book together for you. We even spent one weekend working on it as we made the long drive from Nashville to East Tennessee to visit family, one of us behind the wheel, the other making notes as we talked and reminisced. But these recipes—and the stories behind them—are very much a reflection of who we are now, not just where we've been. We make these foods all the time. They're part of our lives, just as

the people they remind us of always are. In this book, we hope to stir up memories by stirring up some of the best food you've ever tasted.

We're close, and we're family—that's something we're blessed to say. Much of what we associate with family also involves food. We know we aren't alone in that. We were excited by the thought of sharing our love of food and cooking with you and have had more fun than we could've imagined, as you'll see when turning these pages. We have given so much of ourselves to make this book a fun, beautiful, and useful experience for anyone who holds it in their hands.

But this book has given us something unexpected. We knew in our hearts this would be something we would treasure for the rest of our lives, and we will. The time we spent doing this and the process of putting it together has been a joy and a thrill. But it's also brought us even closer. And we have you to thank for that. It was a warm and wonderful experience for us as sisters, and we're hoping you feel the warmth and love we're sending out to you. Do you? Well, good!

Now . . . let's get to doin' some *Good Lookin' Cookin'*! We believe we've earned that title with all of these recipes, and we hope you'll agree. "Bon appétit!" or—as Southern girls say—"Enjoy, y'all!"

About This Book

As you prepare to enjoy and use this book, allow us to share a few notes that you may find helpful. It's important to us that these recipes bring you as much enjoyment as they do us.

We believe every meal has the potential to be like a concert—entertaining, full of color, exciting. An experience, from the minute someone walks in the door—before the curtain even goes up—until the last plate has been cleared and chairs are pushed back from the table. There may even be a light show and some pyro (as you'll see in February and December)!

That's why each menu we're sharing begins with an "Opening Act," an appetizer or snack that sets the stage, getting everyone warmed up for the main attraction. Like Dolly when she's center stage surrounded by top-notch musicians who make her performances come to life, each main dish is supported by a lineup of sides and vegetables that are wonderful on their own yet also make the entire meal shine. And because we know the "audience" gathered around your table is going to want one from you after all that, you'll always be ready for an "Encore" with a picture-perfect dessert.

Like at any good concert, we've added a few unexpected moments for you, too. In some cases, a beverage may precede the "Opening Act" to provide a little pre-show entertainment. And you'll see and hear a "Side Note" now and then where we felt it might add a little something—handy tips for preparing items in advance, storing food, or just managing your "set list" so that every dish strikes the perfect chord and arrives on the stage that is your table the minute it's supposed to.

Helpful Hints

There are some standard terms and basics worth noting that are constant throughout our recipes.

- Rachel often uses sea salt in lieu of kosher or table salt in making these recipes. We didn't specify, unless necessary, knowing people have different tastes and possible dietary needs when it comes to salt.
- "Pepper" is black pepper unless otherwise noted. Freshly ground black pepper is always wonderful if time allows.
- "Sugar" is granulated (white) sugar unless otherwise noted.
- It is safe to assume any egg should be a large egg, unless noted.
- We use salted butter, unless noted—it's just the way we were raised. But these recipes don't specify, allowing you to make your own choice.
- We use whole milk, whole buttermilk, and real cream, especially when it comes to baking. Again, it's how we were raised—it's just a part of us.
- If we list an item as "chopped," we picture that resulting in ½- to ¾-inch pieces. "Diced" would yield ¼- to ½-inch pieces. "Minced" would be smaller than "diced."
- Rachel's go-to choice in cooking is the Texas sweet onion, but yellow or white onions can be used in any recipe requiring onion.
- Many of the dressings included in these recipes and even some of the dips are fantastic as stand-alone dressings for all sorts of salads or fresh vegetables.
- Unless specified, ground beef does not need to be an 80/20 (80% lean, 20% fat) blend.
- Unless noted, "cornmeal mix" can be any boxed blend you like or prefer. We often use Martha White or White Lily brands.
- There is a difference between "stock" and "broth." Stock is richer, more full-bodied, and packed with flavor. We use it often for that reason, but for some recipes, broth will do! We make specific mentions of each where needed.

January

Happy New Year—Let's Get Cookin'!

Happy New Year—Let's Get Cookin'!

The arrival of a new year is celebrated differently in many parts of the world, but in our homes it always includes a traditional New Year's Day meal. We're Southerners, and in the South the first day of the year always involves some version of black-eyed peas that simmer on the stove—usually with ham or bacon—for a good part of the day.

The belief is that eating black-eyed peas—some people call them cowpeas—will bring you good luck and prosperity in the coming year. And they're usually part of a meal that includes pork of some sort and cooked greens. We grew up with all these things, and we continue those traditions with family and friends all these years later. If you're from the South, you have to!

We grew up surrounded by traditions and by family. Our daddy used to keep a silver dollar in his gun rack. Every New Year's Day, Mama would cook a big pot of black-eyed peas, and Daddy would drop that coin into the kettle. Most people would use a dime or a penny, but not Daddy! He used that same silver dollar every year. It came out, went into the pot, Mama would wash it off after the meal, and Daddy would put it away again until the next year.

It didn't make us rich, but we ate like we were. Thanks to Mama and Daddy, we always ate well and had enough. And we learned how to cook and to enjoy the food we make.

Champagne Cocktail

prep time: 5 minutes
makes 1 cocktail

In the South, it's not uncommon at any kind of special meal for the menfolk to have a moonshine cocktail. Everybody celebrates in their own way—it's just a matter of taste—but we think it's great having Champagne with black-eyed peas (see page 27) and greens (see page 28). You can get your cocktail ready, enjoy it, and then invite your family and friends in for one of their own! We like to say, "May the only pain you feel be the Champagne in your glass!"

— Dolly & Rachel

1 sugar cube

2 or 3 drops of aromatic bitters

1 tablespoon cognac

4 ounces Champagne, chilled

Orange peel, for garnish

1 Place the sugar cube in a champagne glass. Drop the bitters into the glass and add cognac. Pour in the Champagne and garnish with the orange peel.

2 Drink immediately, then let your family in. 😉

Opening Act: Chicken Feed

prep time: 10 minutes plus 30 minutes chilling • cook time: 5 minutes
makes 4 servings

Friends gave us this recipe years ago, and it's something we've loved ever since. We just had to put it in the book because it's so good! Chicken Feed is like a small meal—it's a wonderful, hearty little snack for after school but great for company, too. People just love it with drinks, but it goes with pretty much anything.

—Dolly & Rachel

3 English muffins, split and quartered

⅓ cup Kraft Old English sharp pasteurized process cheese spread

¼ cup (½ stick) butter, softened

1 tablespoon Hellmann's or Best Foods mayonnaise

1 (5-ounce) can chicken breast meat, drained

½ teaspoon Morton Nature's Seasons seasoning blend

1. Place the English muffin pieces (24 triangles), split-side up, on a baking sheet. In a medium bowl, use the back of a spoon to combine the cheese spread, butter, mayonnaise, chicken breast, and seasoning blend until you have a creamy consistency.
2. Place 1 rounded teaspoon of the mixture on each muffin triangle. Cover with plastic wrap and chill in the refrigerator for at least 30 minutes or up to 1 hour.
3. After chilling the triangles, adjust the top oven rack so that it's a couple of inches away from the broiler and turn the broiler to high.
4. Broil the triangles for 5 minutes (watch carefully; these can go from browned to burnt pretty quickly) until the edges are browned and the centers are bubbly. Remove from the oven, allow to cool 3 minutes, and serve.

side note Kraft Old English sharp pasteurized process cheese spread and Hellmann's/Best Foods mayonnaise are essential to this; it won't taste the same if you change the recipe. Trust us!

Country Ham and Biscuits

prep time for biscuits: 10 minutes • cook time for biscuits: 15 minutes
prep time for ham: 5 minutes • cook time for ham: 5 minutes
makes 6 servings

We admit it—we love the way butter or some sort of grease makes food taste, especially bacon grease. That's why we use it to cook up country ham. I use it more than Rachel, so I have people save their bacon grease for me. I tell them, "Don't throw away your bacon grease!" And when somebody says, "How do you keep your skin looking so good?" I tell them, "Bacon grease . . . from the inside out!"

— Dolly

This is one of my favorite recipes from many years ago, and it is still a fantastic biscuit! Also, these are so easy to start in the food processor, which I often use to save time. If you don't have one, you can also mix your dry ingredients and cut in your shortening and butter by hand like Mama used to. She was so good at cooking and making biscuits that she could just work the dough by hand and before you knew it, the whole pan would be coming out of the oven!

— Rachel

Buttermilk Biscuits

¼ cup shortening, plus more for greasing

3 cups all-purpose flour, preferably King Arthur (see Side Notes), plus more for dusting

1 tablespoon sugar

1 tablespoon baking powder

1 teaspoon salt

½ teaspoon cream of tartar

½ cup (1 stick) butter, very cold and cut into ½-inch pieces

1¼ cups whole buttermilk, well shaken

Ham

1 teaspoon bacon grease or shortening

3 slices country ham, fat left on

1 To make the biscuits, preheat the oven to 425°F. Grease an 8-inch cast-iron skillet or a similar-size baking pan with shortening.

2 In a large bowl or the bowl of a food processor fitted with the blade attachment, sift together the flour, sugar, baking powder, salt, and cream of tartar. Mix or process a few times to thoroughly combine the dry ingredients.

3 Cut the butter and shortening into the flour mixture by hand using a pastry cutter or pulse them in the food processor just until you get a crumbly consistency. If you're using a food processor, transfer the dough to a large bowl. Add the buttermilk to the bowl and gently stir until just combined, being careful not to overmix.

4 Place the dough on a floured work surface and, with floured hands, gently pat the dough to a 2-inch thickness. Using a 2½-inch biscuit cutter, cut out 6 to 8 biscuits. Transfer to the greased skillet or baking pan, arranging to fit. Bake until golden brown, 12 to 15 minutes. Remove the biscuits from the oven and allow to cool 5 minutes.

5 While the biscuits are baking, make the ham. Add the grease or shortening to a cast-iron skillet. Do not trim any fat from the ham before frying. Melt the grease over medium heat, then add ham slices to the skillet. Fry over medium heat until the edges are brown, a few minutes per side. Remove the ham from the skillet and place the slices on a paper towel–lined plate to drain. Cut the ham slices in half.

6 To serve, split each biscuit in half and sandwich a piece of ham between the top and bottom.

side notes

Country ham is salt-cured ham that's precut, prepackaged, and available at most grocery stores.

I've made these biscuits with many brands of flour, but they really do turn out best with King Arthur.

—Rachel

Pot of Black-Eyed Peas

prep time: 5 minutes • cook time: 1 hour 5 minutes
makes 6 servings

Everybody has a tradition, but nearly everyone in the South believes that you have to have some black-eyed peas to start the new year. It's supposed to bring you good luck. If you don't eat peas, you're not going to have the good luck you might—it's that simple. We included these to make sure your year is as good as ours.

— Dolly & Rachel

3 cups dried black-eyed peas, rinsed well and picked over for any stones

1 medium onion, chopped

1 smoked ham hock, or 1 (¼-pound) slab bacon

1 garlic clove, minced

Salt and pepper to taste

1 Place the black-eyed peas and onion in a medium pot or Dutch oven with the ham hock or bacon slab, adding enough water to cover by an inch. Bring the pot to a boil over high heat, then turn down the heat to medium, cover, and cook for 45 minutes. Add the garlic and salt and pepper. Stir again to combine and simmer, uncovered, for another 20 minutes, or until the peas are tender.

2 If you're using a ham hock, remove it from the pot. Once it has cooled, pull the meat from the bone and return the meat to the pot. Discard the bone.

3 If you're using bacon, remove it from the pot, cut it into chunks, and return it to the pot.

4 Continue simmering the peas, uncovered, until the liquid has thickened and is reduced to about 2 cups, at least 10 minutes more.

side note

Using a fork, you can mash a few peas in the pot and stir them around to thicken the broth.

Turnip Greens

prep time: 15 minutes • cook time: 1 hour
makes 6 servings

We love greens, and grew them back home. The biggest part of cooking any kind of greens is just washing them, rinsing them, washing them, soaking them, rinsing them. We used to say, "Get in there and look them greens," which just meant to look them over good. Mustard, collard—they all taste great—but turnip greens were our favorite because we also used the turnip itself—at least two—for a bit of added flavor. We love that taste.

— Dolly & Rachel

2 bunches turnip greens

3 to 4 tablespoons bacon grease

1 small onion, finely chopped

2 garlic cloves, finely chopped

2 slices country ham, cut into small pieces

3 cups chicken stock, plus more as needed

2 medium turnips, peeled and chopped

1 tablespoon apple cider vinegar

½ teaspoon red pepper flakes (optional)

Salt and pepper to taste

1. Turnip greens need to be washed and picked over well. Put the bundles of turnip greens in a sink with running water and wash them thoroughly. Pull the tough stem from the center of each leaf and discard it. Fill the sink with fresh cold water and press the leaves down into the water, rinsing the greens. Drain the sink, rinsing the sand and dirt from the bottom of the sink down the drain. Refill the sink with cold water and rinse again. Repeat the process four times total until your greens are completely free of dirt and sand. Place the greens in a large colander to drain.

2. In a large pot or Dutch oven over medium-high heat, warm the bacon grease. Add the onion, garlic, and ham and cook until the onion is translucent and the ham is lightly golden, 4 to 6 minutes. Add the chicken stock, stir to deglaze the pot, and bring to a boil.

3. Add the turnips first, then layer the greens into the pot. It may initially appear as though there are too many greens for the pot to hold, but they will quickly wilt. Once they are wilted, add the vinegar and red pepper flakes (if desired). If needed, add more chicken stock, so the liquid cooks down but never boils dry. Lower the heat to medium and cook, uncovered, for 45 minutes to 1 hour, until the greens are tender. Season with salt and pepper and serve.

Skillet Cornbread

prep time: 10 minutes • cook time: 25 minutes
makes 6 servings

Everyone needs a good cast-iron skillet. In the South, it's not uncommon for a bride to receive one as a wedding gift—and not always a new one! One of the best traditions we enjoy is when a well-used, well-seasoned cast-iron skillet is handed down through the generations, like our Mama's were. We both still have—and use—skillets of hers that have made cornbread more times than we'll ever know.

—Dolly & Rachel

5 tablespoons bacon grease or shortening

2 cups Martha White or White Lily self-rising buttermilk-enriched white cornmeal mix

1½ cups whole buttermilk, well shaken

1 teaspoon salt

¼ teaspoon pepper

1 Preheat the oven to 400°F. Heat the bacon grease or shortening on the stovetop in a well-seasoned 8-inch cast-iron skillet over medium heat until smoking hot. Remove from the burner.

2 In a large bowl, whisk together the cornmeal mix, buttermilk, salt, and pepper. Add 2 tablespoons of the hot grease or shortening to the batter and mix well. Pour the batter into the hot skillet—it will sizzle a bit on the sides, but that's good! Place the skillet in the oven and bake until golden brown, about 25 minutes.

3 Remove the cornbread from oven and let cool for 10 minutes in the pan. Slice and serve.

Encore: Chocolate Pie with Meringue

prep time for homemade pie crust: 15 minutes plus 1 hour chilling
cook time: 16 minutes
prep time for chocolate pie: 15 minutes plus 20 minutes cooling
cook time: 10 minutes
makes 8 servings

This really is "good lookin' cookin'," especially when Rachel makes it with the little peaks of brown meringue on top. When I was young, I was one of those kids that stands at the oven door opening it a thousand times to see if it's ready.

— Dolly

The secret is the bowl you prep the meringue in. I usually put it in the fridge first and then try to keep everything as cool as possible. Cream of tartar holds things together to make those peaks.

— Rachel

Homemade Pie Crust (makes one 9-inch single pie crust)

1¼ cups all-purpose flour, plus more for dusting

½ teaspoon salt

½ teaspoon sugar

6 tablespoons (¾ stick) cold unsalted butter, thinly sliced

2 tablespoons shortening

⅛ to ¼ cup ice water

Chocolate Pie

1 pie crust (this recipe or store-bought)

1 cup water

¾ cup evaporated milk

4 egg yolks (save whites for making meringue)

1½ cups sugar

¼ cup unsweetened cocoa powder

¼ cup cornstarch

¼ teaspoon salt

¼ cup (½ stick) butter, cubed

Meringue

5 egg whites (4 reserved from pie filling plus 1 extra)

⅓ cup powdered sugar

¼ teaspoon cream of tartar

1 To make the pie crust, place the flour, salt, and sugar in the bowl of a food processor fitted with the blade attachment and process for a few seconds to combine. Add the butter pieces and shortening and process until the mixture is crumbly, about 10 seconds.

continued

WILLIAMS SONOM

Chocolate Pie with Meringue, continued

2 With the machine running, add the ice water in a slow, steady stream through the feed tube just until the dough holds together. Do not overprocess. To check the dough, turn off the food processor. The dough should easily pinch together between your fingers.

3 Turn the dough out onto a sheet of plastic wrap. Flatten to form a disk. Wrap and refrigerate at least 1 hour before rolling.

4 To bake the pie crust, preheat the oven to 350°F. On a lightly floured surface, roll out the dough and press it into a 9-inch pie plate. The dough should exceed the edge by 1 inch. Fold under and crimp the excess dough, using your fingers or the prongs of a fork.

5 Prick the pie crust lightly all over with the prongs of a fork. Line the crust with parchment paper and fill with pie weights or dried beans. Bake the pie crust until lightly browned, 12 to 16 minutes. (For store-bought pie crust, follow the baking instructions on the package.) Let the crust cool 20 to 30 minutes, then remove the pie weights.

6 To make the pie filling, in a medium bowl, whisk together the water, evaporated milk, and egg yolks, stirring until smooth and combined. In an 8-inch cast-iron skillet, mix the sugar, cocoa powder, cornstarch, and salt, stirring until combined. Place the skillet over medium-high heat. Pour in the wet ingredients while stirring constantly and cook until thickened, 6 to 8 minutes. Do not allow the mixture to boil.

7 Remove the skillet from the heat and add the butter, stirring to melt. When the butter has melted, allow the mixture to cool for 20 minutes. Pour the mixture into the baked crust. Set aside and make the meringue.

8 To make the meringue, preheat the oven to 375°F.

9 In a large chilled bowl and using an electric hand mixer, or in a stand mixer fitted with the paddle attachment, beat the egg whites on medium speed until frothy and smooth, about 2 minutes. Add the powdered sugar and cream of tartar and continue beating on medium speed until stiff peaks form, another 2 to 4 minutes. Cover the pie with the meringue, using a spoon to make swirls and peaks. Bake the pie just until the meringue peaks begin to brown, about 5 minutes.

side note

The trick to making a tender, flaky pie crust is not to handle it too much and to be stingy with the flour when you're rollin' it out.

February

Valentine's Day—Eat Your Heart Out

XOXO

Valentine's Day—Eat Your Heart Out

We learned a lot from Mama and Daddy, especially about love.

On Valentine's Day, they had their special things, just as they did at Christmas. There was always a box of candy and handkerchiefs. Mama would give Daddy handkerchiefs, and he'd give her a box of chocolate-covered cherries that they would share.

Daddy and Mama would have loved the recipes in this chapter, even though several of them are things we never could've imagined making and enjoying when we were younger. They are dishes we now share with our husbands or make for our families.

We love Valentine's Day—it's a special day for each of us and our sweethearts. Through the years we have often gone out to celebrate, but we also cook a meal like this at home.

There's lots to love in this meal. Valentine's Day is the perfect occasion to use your kitchen to create dishes you may associate with dining out. Whether it's a special appetizer, a main dish that you may not get to enjoy often, or a restaurant-caliber dessert, we enjoy doing a little something extra for ourselves and our special someones. With these recipes, you can, too.

Opening Act: Stuffed Mushrooms

prep time: 15 minutes • cook time: 15 minutes
makes 4 to 6 servings

There was a restaurant in New York that I used to go to just to get their stuffed mushrooms. It's out of business, but Rachel's version tastes just like what I had there!

— Dolly

This recipe is simple and easy, making it a wonderful appetizer. And I just love mushrooms. We both do!

— Rachel

1 tablespoon extra-virgin olive oil, for greasing

3 tablespoons butter, melted

3 tablespoons minced onion

1 garlic clove, minced

½ cup Italian bread crumbs

¼ cup grated Parmesan cheese

2 tablespoons chopped fresh parsley

12 large white button mushrooms, cleaned with stems removed

1. Preheat the oven to 350°F. Grease a rimmed baking sheet or a baking pan with the olive oil.
2. In a large bowl, mix together the melted butter, onion, garlic, bread crumbs, Parmesan cheese, and parsley. Stuff each mushroom cap with 1 teaspoon of filling.
3. Place the stuffed mushrooms on the prepared baking sheet. Bake until the filling is golden brown and the mushroom caps are tender, about 15 minutes. Serve warm.

Steak and Lobster with Drawn Butter

prep time: 15 minutes • cook time: 20 minutes
makes 4 servings

Don't be intimidated by lobster. It may cost a little extra and feel like a splurge, but don't be afraid. It can be prepared many ways, but broiling it is a breeze. "Surf and turf" is the ultimate meal when you go out—the combination and tastes complement each other so well. Just try it—it's wonderful made at home!

—Dolly & Cathy

Steak

4 (8-ounce) steaks (filet mignon or cut of your choice)
Extra-virgin olive oil
1 teaspoon salt
1 teaspoon pepper
1 teaspoon garlic powder
¼ cup (½ stick) butter, cut into 1-tablespoon portions

Lobster

4 lobster tails
½ cup (1 stick) butter
1 teaspoon minced garlic
½ teaspoon salt
¼ teaspoon pepper
1 lemon, cut into 4 wedges

Drawn Butter

1 cup (2 sticks) butter

1 Preheat the oven to 500°F.

2 To prepare the steak, place the filets on a large plate. Brush each lightly on both sides with olive oil. Season both sides with equal parts salt, pepper, and garlic powder. Let the meat sit at room temperature for 30 minutes. Heat an 8- to 10-inch cast-iron skillet over medium-high heat until it just begins to smoke. Make sure you have proper ventilation, like a vent over the cooktop.

3 When the skillet begins to smoke, sear the steaks until just browned, about 2 minutes, then flip to sear the other side until browned, 2 minutes more. Place the skillet in the oven for 2 minutes for medium-rare doneness, 5 minutes for medium doneness, or 7 minutes for well done. Remove the skillet from the oven and place the steaks on a clean plate.

continued

Steak and Lobster with Drawn Butter, continued

4 Top each steak with a pat of butter (about 1 tablespoon). Tent the plate with aluminum foil, leaving the sides vented so steam can escape. Let the steaks rest for 5 to 10 minutes.

5 To prepare the lobster, adjust the top oven rack so that it's just a couple inches below the broiler. Turn the broiler to high.

6 Holding a lobster tail, use sharp kitchen shears to cut down the middle of the shell toward the end of the tail. Place the lobster tail on a rimmed baking sheet or in a 9 by 13-inch baking dish. Using your fingers, pull the shell apart down the middle to expose the lobster meat. Repeat with the remaining lobster tails.

7 In a small saucepan over medium heat, melt the stick of butter. Add the garlic, salt, and pepper and whisk to combine. Pour the seasoned butter over the lobster meat. Broil until the meat is white and the tail is bright pink, watching carefully (as broilers vary), 7 to 10 minutes. If you have a meat thermometer, the center of the meat should register 145°F.

8 While the lobster is in the oven, make the drawn butter. In the small saucepan over medium heat, melt the two sticks of butter. Turn down the temperature to low and continue to cook until the butterfat becomes very clear and the whitish milk solids drop to the bottom of the pan.

9 Skim the surface foam as the butter clarifies and dispose of it. Evenly divide and ladle the clarified butter from the saucepan into four ramekins, one for each place setting.

10 Serve each lobster tail with a lemon wedge and drawn butter. Plate with the steak and a baked potato (page 48).

side note

If your family is anything like ours, then you'll want to have A.1. steak sauce on the table to go with this. In family photos taken through the years, it's clear that we always have it on hand!

BE MY VALENTINE

Garden Salad with Miracle Madness Dressing

prep time: 10 minutes
makes 4 servings

I've always loved the taste of Miracle Whip, and this is a salad I've made for years. When Rachel and different family members come by, they always ask me to make my special salad. The little bit of sugar is kind of my special ingredient. It's no secret now, though—all of our secrets are coming out in this book!

—Dolly

1 cup Miracle Whip
1 tablespoon lemon juice
1 tablespoon sugar
½ teaspoon salt
½ teaspoon pepper
1 head iceberg lettuce, washed, dried, and chopped
1 large tomato, chopped

In a small bowl, combine the Miracle Whip, lemon juice, sugar, salt, and pepper. Place the lettuce in a large serving bowl. Pour the dressing over the lettuce and toss until well coated. Cover the bowl and place the salad in the refrigerator until ready to serve. Just before serving, top with the chopped tomato.

side note
We use a lettuce spinner to dry the iceberg lettuce—it works so well!

Baked Potato

prep time: 10 minutes • cook time: 1 hour
makes 4 servings

We love a loaded baked potato. Our way of preparing these is a little different, but it works. After that, it's up to you what you add—there are so many toppings to try. The simple fact is, there's no wrong way to serve one, even if you simply like your potatoes plain and hot out of the oven!

—Dolly & Rachel

4 medium russet potatoes

¼ cup (½ stick) butter, cut into 1-tablespoon portions

Optional Toppings

Shredded cheese of your choice

Sour cream

Bacon, cooked and finely chopped

Green onion, chopped

Salt and pepper to taste

1 Preheat the oven to 450°F. Scrub the potatoes under running water, then dry them completely. (We usually air-dry them on a paper towel, because our favorite way to bake them is directly on the oven rack, and to do this they need to be fully dry and unpierced. The skins crisp up nicely when they're baked this way.) Place on a rack in the oven and bake 45 minutes to 1 hour. To check for doneness, pierce the center with a knife. If it's soft, they're done.

2 Remove the potatoes from the oven. Slice down the middle. Top with the butter, followed by other items (as desired) for a loaded potato.

side note If your family is like ours, you're going to need extra butter!

Encore: Light My Fire Bananas Foster

prep time: 5 minutes • cook time: 10 minutes
makes 4 servings

We have always been fascinated by seeing desserts or drinks lit on fire in restaurants. Sometimes you don't know whether to eat it or drink it or run! If you don't feel comfortable using rum in this and lighting it, that's okay—put yours in a glass and enjoy sipping it.

— Dolly & Rachel

4 firm medium bananas

¼ cup (½ stick) butter

1 cup packed light brown sugar

1 teaspoon vanilla extract

½ teaspoon ground cinnamon

3 tablespoons dark rum (optional)

Vanilla ice cream, for serving

1 Peel the bananas and slice lengthwise, then set aside. Melt the butter in an 8- or 10-inch skillet over medium-low heat. Stir in the brown sugar, vanilla, and cinnamon. Cook, stirring often, until the sugar dissolves, 3 to 4 minutes. If you're going to "light my fire," this is when you do it! (But have a lid close by just in case!) Use a small kitchen hand torch for the task or a long stick lighter. Add the rum to the skillet and light it—the alcohol in the rum should burn just briefly, and then the flame will go out.

2 Turn down the heat to low and add the banana slices. Gently flip them, coating them in the liquid, and cook until heated through and just beginning to soften, about 2 minutes.

3 Place two banana slices and one scoop of ice cream in each dish. Top with warm sauce from the skillet and serve.

side note Every kitchen should have a fire extinguisher. This would be a good occasion to make sure yours has one!

March

St. Patrick's Day ~ A Few Lucky Charms

St. Patrick's Day—A Few Lucky Charms

Lots of things come to mind for us when we think of March—there's St. Patrick's Day, of course, and we also think a lot about Daddy, who was born in March. It was a busy time of year—he and our brothers would burn the tobacco beds throughout the month, which fertilized the land and got it ready for planting. With spring about to begin, it was time to plant new tobacco, which was Daddy's main money crop. All that work made for some hungry mouths that Mama had to feed.

Hearty dishes cooked low and slow, like pot roast or corned beef, are the kind of things Daddy always enjoyed this time of year. He loved sauerkraut, too. We've found creative ways for you to serve and enjoy these dishes as well, through recipes that allow you to transform a traditional St. Patrick's Day main dish into a meal to celebrate the holiday, complete with a little bit of green at the start and finish.

Green Beer

prep time: 5 minutes
makes 1 serving

We really enjoy a Guinness with this meal, but the truth is we've tried and just can't make Guinness—even the lighter ones—turn the right shade of green, so we use light beer to set the tone. Enjoy one of these, then move on to Guinness!

— Dolly & Rachel

1 (12-ounce) light beer (the lighter the better)

Green liquid food coloring

Pour the beer into a glass. Add a few drops of food coloring—as much as needed—to turn the beer green. Stir gently and serve.

Miller
HIGH
HIGH

Opening Act: Shamrock Sauerkraut Balls

prep time: 20 minutes plus 1 hour chilling • cook time: 4 minutes
makes about 32 sauerkraut balls

This is an old recipe, but the food processor makes it "new." We love using our food processors, and this is a perfect example why. It chops up the sauerkraut and the meat so well that the appetizers turn out perfect when you form and shape them. Just make sure to refrigerate so they hold that shape when you put them in the deep fryer!

—Dolly & Rachel

1 slice rye bread

4 slices deli corned beef

1 cup mashed potatoes (Idahoan brand instant single-serve cups are perfect for this if you don't have leftover mashed potatoes on hand)

2 slices deli Swiss cheese

2 tablespoons Thousand Island dressing, plus more for serving

2 teaspoons caraway seeds

1 teaspoon Dijon mustard

½ cup drained sauerkraut

Peanut oil or canola oil, for frying

2 eggs

1 cup panko bread crumbs

1 Line a rimmed baking sheet with parchment paper. Place the rye bread in a food processor fitted with the blade attachment and pulse until it's turned to bread crumbs. Transfer to a small bowl.

2 To the same food processor, add the corned beef, mashed potatoes, Swiss cheese, Thousand Island dressing, caraway seeds, and Dijon mustard. Add the sauerkraut to the food processor along with the rye bread crumbs. Pulse all ingredients until well combined and a uniform consistency. Using a small cookie scoop or tablespoon measure, create bite-size 1-inch rounds and place them on the prepared baking sheet. Cover with plastic wrap and refrigerate for at least 1 hour.

3 When you're ready to fry, fill a deep fryer or large Dutch oven with 3 to 4 inches of oil and heat over medium-high heat until a deep-fry thermometer reaches 350°F.

4 In a medium bowl, beat the eggs. Spread the panko bread crumbs on a plate. Remove the sauerkraut balls from the refrigerator. Dip each one in the egg wash, then roll in the panko.

5 Using a fry basket or spider strainer, fry the sauerkraut balls until golden brown, 2 to 4 minutes. Drain on a plate lined with paper towels and then transfer to a serving plate. Provide toothpicks and serve with a side of Thousand Island dressing for dipping.

Corned Beef Brisket with Carrots, Cabbage, and Potatoes

prep time: 15 minutes • cook time: 2 hours 30 minutes
makes 6 servings

This is so much easier to make than people think. Just because you don't have something every day, or maybe make it only once a year, doesn't mean you should think you can't. Store-bought corned beef is ready to be cooked—just put the seasonings and everything together. It takes time—you have to cook it low and slow—but the results are delicious.

—Dolly & Rachel

1 (3-pound) corned beef brisket and accompanying spice packet

1 teaspoon coarse black pepper

2 bay leaves

2 medium russet potatoes, peeled and quartered

3 medium carrots, peeled and quartered

1 medium onion, quartered

1 medium head green cabbage, cored and quartered into wedges

Dijon mustard, prepared horseradish, and sour cream, for serving (optional)

1 Rinse the corned beef under cool water and pat it dry. Place the brisket in a large Dutch oven, add the contents of the spice packet, pepper, bay leaves, and 4 cups water and bring to a boil over medium-high heat. Reduce the heat, cover, and simmer until the meat is fork-tender, about 2 hours.

2 Add the potatoes, carrots, and onion to the brisket and bring it back to a boil over medium-high heat. Reduce the heat once more to a simmer, cover, and cook for 10 minutes. Lastly, add the cabbage and continue to simmer, covered, until all the vegetables are tender, about 20 minutes more.

3 Discard the bay leaves. Transfer the meat to a cutting board, let rest 5 minutes, then slice it, placing the slices on a serving plate. Add the vegetables to the plate using a slotted spoon. Serve with small ramekins of mustard, horseradish, and sour cream, if you like.

Cast-Iron Cornbread Sticks

prep time: 10 minutes • cook time: 18 minutes
makes 6 servings

We don't make sweet cornbread as much as some people do. Mountain people usually didn't sweeten cornbread because poor families couldn't afford sugar. We were usually without it, but we can cook it that way if somebody wants. It's just like adding an egg to the cornbread—sometimes you do, sometimes you don't. This recipe has both sugar and an egg! All you need is a shaped baking pan to create sticks as a serving variation. Ours are cast iron, but there are metal and silicone options, too.

— Dolly & Rachel

3 tablespoons vegetable oil or canola oil (½ tablespoon per corn-stick well)

1 cup plus 2 tablespoons yellow cornmeal

2 tablespoons all-purpose flour

2 tablespoons sugar (optional)

1 teaspoon salt

1 teaspoon baking powder

1 egg

½ cup whole buttermilk, well shaken

1 tablespoon butter, melted

1 Preheat the oven to 400°F. Grease the corn-stick pan with the oil and place the pan in the oven while you make the batter.

2 In a medium bowl, combine the cornmeal, flour, sugar (if using), salt, and baking powder and stir to blend. In a separate medium bowl, whisk together the egg, buttermilk, and melted butter until smooth and combined. Stir the wet mixture into the dry ingredients to create a thick batter, but don't overwork it.

3 Remove the corn-stick pan from the oven. Careful—it will be *very* hot! Evenly divide and spoon the batter into each well just until full—do not overfill. Bake until golden brown, about 18 minutes. Serve warm or at room temperature.

side note

Since this can be made as a sweetened cornbread if desired, you can try Dolly Parton's Sweet Cornbread and Muffin Mix from Duncan Hines for a quick and different take on this! It'll yield 12 cornbread sticks or 1 (10-inch) skillet cornbread.

Encore: Irish Dream Cake

prep time: 30 minutes • cook time: 40 minutes
makes 8 to 10 servings

This is a wonderful white cake. On its own, it's perfectly enjoyable, with a light, subtle taste. We add green gel food coloring to the batter to create our Irish Dream dessert, and the batter takes the color beautifully. It can be great fun taking something simple and—with just a little creativity—turning it into so much more!

Cake

Shortening, for greasing

1 cup (2 sticks) butter, softened

2 cups sugar

5 egg whites

3 cups sifted all-purpose flour, plus more for dusting

1 cup whole milk, room temperature

1½ teaspoons vanilla extract

1 teaspoon green gel food coloring

Cream Cheese Frosting

2 (8-ounce) blocks cream cheese, room temperature

½ cup (1 stick) butter, softened

1½ teaspoons vanilla extract

2 cups powdered sugar

Green sugar sprinkles

1 To make the cake, preheat the oven to 350°F. Prepare two 2-inch-deep by 8-inch round cake pans by greasing them with shortening and lightly dusting each with flour.

2 In a large bowl and using an electric hand mixer, or in a stand mixer fitted with a paddle attachment, cream together the butter and sugar until light and fluffy, 2 to 3 minutes. Add the egg whites a little at a time, beating after each addition, until thoroughly combined. Add the flour, milk, vanilla, and food coloring and mix well.

3 Divide the batter evenly between the two prepared pans. Bake on the center rack for 35 to 40 minutes. Test by inserting a wooden toothpick into the center of the cake; if the toothpick comes out clean, the cake is done. If it's not done, return it to the oven and bake an additional 2 to 3 minutes.

4 Remove the pans from the oven and place them on a cooling rack to cool for 8 minutes. Gently turn out the cakes onto the rack and allow them to cool completely.

5 If you would like more of the green color to show in each piece of cake, you can cut the bottom and outer browned edges off of the cakes once they're completely cooled. To trim the cakes, transfer each cake to a cutting board, bottom-side down. Using

a long serrated knife held in your dominant hand, firmly place your other hand on top of the cake and saw back and forth in an even motion until the knife comes out the other side, skimming the top off the cake. Take off the thin top of the cake and discard (or enjoy as a snack). With a paring knife, gently trim the outer baked edge all the way around and lift it away from the cake. Transfer the cake to a cake plate. Repeat with the second layer but do not stack the two cakes until you're ready to assemble and frost.

6 To make the frosting, in a large bowl and using an electric hand mixer, or in a stand mixer fitted with a paddle attachment, beat the cream cheese, butter, vanilla, and powdered sugar until light and fluffy, 2 to 3 minutes.

7 When you're ready to assemble the cake, spread approximately half of the frosting onto the first cake layer. Place the second cake layer on top and finish by spreading the remaining frosting over the top and sides until evenly coated. Decorate with green sugar sprinkles.

side note

If you have leftover frosting, store it in the refrigerator in an airtight container. You can use it again at room temperature with fresh strawberries. Coat each strawberry with frosting, then roll them in miniature chocolate chip morsels.

April

Easter—Bunny's Delight

Easter—Bunny's Delight

No matter where Easter falls on the calendar, it's always a special time of year. Everything is turning green, flowers are blooming, and the sun is warmer as it shines through the windows. It's springtime—a time of rebirth when everything is new again.

It's also a time in our family for gathering to celebrate the occasion. We grew up in a Christian family, and the meaning of Easter—that Christ has risen—is important to us. Our grandpa was a preacher, and he made certain we were reminded what Easter is really about before we enjoyed our big Easter meal.

But that doesn't mean our holiday didn't include all the things so many people associate with Easter. And it still does. The kids—our nieces and nephews—dye and color eggs. We have Dressed Eggs on our tables (our grandpa didn't like mentioning the word *devil*), fresh spring asparagus in the oven, and Coconut Cake on a stand, covered in buttercream and coconut flakes, ready to delight everyone for dessert. And though it may not be a traditional choice, the chicken and dumplin's that have always been such a big part of our lives are the perfect centerpiece for a springtime meal. There are few dishes that say "family" to us the way they do.

Opening Act: Fried Green Tomatoes with Ranch Dressing

prep time: 15 minutes • cook time: 15 minutes
makes 6 to 8 servings of the tomatoes and enough dressing to fill a 16-ounce mason jar

Rachel's version of this really is "good lookin' cookin'," but I make mine like Mama did. She had this house full of kids and everything that comes with that, so her fried green tomatoes would sometimes end up in pieces, like fried potatoes, as she flipped them. That's how I make mine. But we wanted to share Rachel's recipe, because it's so pretty and delicious.

— Dolly

This is a wonderful recipe, really. It's easy. And homemade dressings are, too. Using this one with dip for an appetizer is so much fun and so good. If you can get green tomatoes at a farmers' market or grow them yourself, this is the perfect recipe for you. I love to pick them when they're just beginning to ripen, because I find it adds a little sweetness to this!

— Rachel

Ranch Dressing

1 cup mayonnaise

½ cup sour cream

¼ cup whole buttermilk

1 tablespoon chopped fresh chives

1 tablespoon chopped fresh parsley

1 tablespoon chopped fresh dill

1 teaspoon minced fresh garlic

½ teaspoon salt

½ teaspoon pepper

Fried Green Tomatoes

Peanut or canola oil, for frying

2 cups cornmeal mix

1 teaspoon salt

1 teaspoon pepper

1 teaspoon garlic powder

1 teaspoon onion powder

2 eggs

¼ cup whole milk

5 large green tomatoes, cored and cut into ¼- to ½-inch-thick slices

1 To make the ranch dressing, in a medium bowl, whisk together the mayonnaise, sour cream, buttermilk, chives, parsley, dill, garlic, salt, and pepper until smooth. Place it in an airtight container if you're making it in advance. The dressing will keep in the refrigerator for up to 1 week.

continued

Fried Green Tomatoes, continued

2 To fry the tomatoes, prepare a deep fryer according to the manufacturer's instructions and heat to 375°F. We like to use peanut oil, but canola oil is a good alternative. Preheat the oven to the lowest possible temperature setting for warming. Line a baking sheet with paper towels.

3 In a pie plate, combine the cornmeal mix, salt, pepper, garlic powder, and onion powder. In a second pie plate, make an egg wash by whisking together the eggs and milk.

4 Dip one tomato slice at a time into the egg wash and then into the cornmeal mixture, turning to coat both sides. Line the bottom of the fryer basket with the tomato slices (making sure not to layer them). Fry in batches, one basket at a time, until golden brown, 3 to 4 minutes. Empty the basket onto the prepared baking sheet to drain. Continue frying the remaining tomato slices.

5 Keep the tomatoes warm in the oven on a wire rack placed inside a rimmed baking sheet until ready to serve. Serve with ranch dressing for dipping.

side note

If you don't have a deep fryer, follow the breading instructions and pan-fry the tomato slices in a large skillet with an inch of peanut oil or canola oil over medium-high heat, turning them to brown and crisp. Don't layer the slices, and don't crowd them. Using a slotted spatula, remove the fried tomatoes and place them on a paper towel-lined baking sheet to drain.

Dressed Eggs

prep time: 25 minutes • cook time: 15 minutes
makes 24 halves

You can "dress" your dressed eggs pretty much any way you like. If you like things a little sweet, finely mince a tablespoon of sweet pickles and add them to the yolk mixture. If you like things savory, add a tablespoon of minced olives to the mixture. Carl (Dolly's husband) likes them simple, so that's how we make them for him, but some of our family members even like chopped bacon on top as a garnish—it's delicious, too. Since it's Easter, wear your best dress and decide how "dressy" *you* want your eggs to be!

— Dolly & Rachel

12 eggs
⅓ cup mayonnaise
1 teaspoon Dijon mustard
3 drops Tabasco sauce
¼ teaspoon salt
Fresh chives, for garnish
Paprika, for garnish

1. Place the eggs in a large saucepan and add just enough water to cover them. Bring to a boil over medium-high heat. Put the lid on the saucepan, reduce the temperature to low, and simmer for 5 minutes. Remove the saucepan from the heat and move eggs to a colander in the sink. Run cold water over the eggs until they're cool enough to handle. Crack the shells by tapping the eggs together gently, then peel and discard the shells.
2. Cut each egg in half lengthwise. Carefully remove the yolks and place them in a small bowl. Using a fork, mash the yolks. Add the mayonnaise, mustard, Tabasco, and salt and blend with the fork until smooth. Place the egg whites on a platter or an egg plate and use two small spoons (one to scoop and one to fill) to fill each egg white half with the yolk mixture.
3. Using small kitchen scissors, cut the chives into small pieces to garnish. Sprinkle with paprika before serving.

Mashed Potatoes

prep time: 10 minutes • cook time: 30 minutes
makes 6 to 8 servings

The fact of the matter is that potatoes have been a part of our lives forever. Daddy grew more potatoes than anything else—we had more potatoes than beans, more potatoes than corn. They were in soups and stews, fried, boiled, and baked. We loved them then, and we love them still. You could say we've never met a potato we didn't like . . . and we sure like these!

— Dolly & Rachel

4 pounds large red potatoes

1½ teaspoons salt

¼ cup (½ stick) butter, plus a pat for serving

¾ cup whole milk, room temperature, plus more as needed

Chopped fresh parsley, for garnish (optional)

1 Wash, scrub, and peel the potatoes. Remove any blemishes. Cut and quarter the potatoes and place them in a colander. Rinse the potatoes under cold running water until it runs clear.

2 Transfer the potatoes to a large pot and cover with cold water. Add 1 teaspoon of the salt and bring to a boil over high heat. Reduce the heat to medium-high and cook until the potatoes are fork-tender, about 20 minutes.

3 Drain the potatoes in a colander, then place them in a large bowl. Using a potato masher or an electric hand mixer, mash the potatoes. (Don't worry if you leave some lumps—they give it texture!) Add the butter, milk, and remaining ½ teaspoon salt and mash further. Add more milk if needed to achieve your desired texture. Finish with the additional pat of butter and garnish with parsley.

Oven-Roasted Asparagus

prep time: 5 minutes • cook time: 15 minutes
makes 6 servings

We love asparagus. You can prepare it so many ways, and we enjoy playing around with combinations like this. Easter is a special occasion, and asparagus is a special reflection of this time of year. Though now it's available in stores year-round, in spring it's fresh, crisp, and flavorful—and easy to prepare!

—Dolly & Rachel

- 1 large or 2 small bundles asparagus, trimmed
- 3 tablespoons extra-virgin olive oil
- 1 tablespoon lemon juice
- 1 teaspoon sea salt
- 1 teaspoon pepper
- 1 garlic clove, minced
- Zest of 1 lemon, for garnish

1. Preheat the oven to 400°F. Arrange the asparagus in a single layer on a baking sheet. In a small bowl, stir together the olive oil, lemon juice, salt, pepper, and garlic. Pour it over the asparagus, turning the spears until they are well coated.
2. Bake until the asparagus is crisp-tender, 12 to 15 minutes (depending on the thickness of the asparagus). Garnish with lemon zest and serve.

Slaw of Many Colors

prep time: 15 minutes plus 2 hours chilling
makes 6 servings

Our grandfather was a preacher, so when we were growing up, the whole family would often join the community for all-day church singing and dinner on the grounds. There was almost always a table covered with food, including bowls of coleslaw. Each one tasted different, because every cook used their own special ingredient. This is ours, and it is full of color—purple and green and red. It's got everything!

—Dolly & Rachel

1 medium head red cabbage, chopped
1 green bell pepper, seeded and chopped
1 medium onion, chopped
1 cup mayonnaise
½ cup apple cider vinegar
½ cup powdered sugar
1 teaspoon salt
1 large tomato, chopped
Salt and pepper to taste

1. Combine the cabbage, bell pepper, and onion in a large bowl. In a small bowl, whisk together the mayonnaise, vinegar, powdered sugar, and salt until smooth. Pour the dressing over the vegetables, tossing well to combine. Cover and refrigerate for at least 2 hours to allow everything to marinate.
2. When ready to serve, gently stir in the chopped tomato and season with salt and pepper.

side note

You can chop all the vegetables except the tomato in a food processor. We like our cabbage chopped, but a few of our sisters prefer to shred or thinly slice it.

Rustic Chicken and Dumplin's

prep time: 30 minutes plus 30 minutes chilling • cook time: 1 hour 15 minutes
makes 4 to 6 servings

I call this rustic because I leave the bones in, which is authentic. But that means you must be careful and make sure not to swallow any! There are so many ways to make this dish, and since our brothers and sisters cook as well, our family has several versions. I often ask the meat department or butcher to hand cut a whole chicken into pieces for me (the backbone and wings can be used later to make stock). This is one of Dolly's favorite dishes, so I usually make it for her birthday in January.

Chicken

- 1 whole chicken, cut into pieces
- Morton Nature's Seasons seasoning blend to taste
- 3 tablespoons butter
- 1 (32-ounce) carton chicken stock
- 2 cups water
- 1 teaspoon poultry seasoning
- 1 teaspoon minced garlic
- 1 teaspoon salt
- 1 teaspoon pepper
- ½ onion, minced
- 3 carrots, cut into 1-inch pieces
- 3 celery stalks, cut into 1-inch pieces
- Chopped fresh parsley, for garnish

Dumplin's

- 1¼ cups all-purpose flour, plus more for dusting
- 1 teaspoon baking powder
- ½ teaspoon salt
- 1 egg
- ¾ cup whole buttermilk, well shaken
- ½ cup (1 stick) cold butter, cut into thin slices

1 To prepare the chicken, rinse it under cold running water and pat the pieces dry with a paper towel. Season it all over with the Morton seasoning blend.

2 In a 12-inch cast-iron skillet or large Dutch oven over medium-high heat, melt the butter. Add the chicken pieces, skin-side down, and cook until golden brown, 6 to 8 minutes. Turn the chicken pieces and brown again for another 6 to 8 minutes.

side note

Rachel always makes this special for me on my birthday. I'm so busy doing other things, I sometimes forget my own birthday until she says, "Come on over!"

—Dolly

continued

Rustic Chicken and Dumplin's, continued

3 Add the chicken stock and water, and bring to a boil over high heat. Lower the heat to medium, add the poultry seasoning, garlic, salt, pepper, and onion, and cover with a lid to simmer for 20 minutes. Add the carrots and celery. Leave the lid ajar, allowing the steam to vent, and keep simmering on low heat until the vegetables are almost tender, about 20 minutes.

4 Meanwhile, make the dumplin's. In a large bowl, sift together the flour, baking powder, and salt. In a medium bowl, whisk the egg with the buttermilk and set aside.

5 Cut the butter into the dry mixture using a pastry cutter (if you don't have one, a fork or two knives will work). Blend well to a crumbly consistency. Add the buttermilk-egg mixture and gently stir with a wooden spoon until combined. Cover with plastic wrap and refrigerate for 30 minutes.

6 Remove the dough from the refrigerator and turn it out onto a floured surface. Using your hands, pat the dough out to about 1-inch thickness and fold it by pulling the outer edges into the center. Gather the edges of the dough with your fingertips and then lift and bring those edges toward the middle. *Gently* fold—do not knead—until it comes together. Pat the dough out again to about a 1-inch thickness.

7 Remove the cooked chicken from the skillet and put it on a plate. Cover it with aluminum foil to keep warm. Bring the broth to a gentle boil over medium-high heat. (Now would be the time, if you'd like, to remove the chicken bones before adding the chicken meat to the broth.)

8 Using a knife, cut the chilled dough into 2-inch squares. Gently drop each square, one at a time, into the boiling broth. Lower the heat to medium and simmer, uncovered, until all of the dumplings rise to the top, about 10 minutes. Return the chicken to the pot and simmer an additional 5 minutes.

9 Using a soup ladle, divide the chicken and dumplin's among individual bowls. Garnish with the parsley and serve.

Encore: Coconut Cake

prep time: 25 minutes plus 1 hour chilling time • cook time: 35 minutes
makes 10 to 12 servings

After we each left home and got married, we started making food that is as pretty as it is tasty. We still take pride in those recipes, and this is one of them. We have to have coconut cake on Easter—with coconut flakes sprinkled on top. It's a tradition. And there's nothing wrong with using a cake mix if you like! Whether you make this as described or use Dolly's Southern Style Coconut Flavored Cake Mix from Duncan Hines for a cupcake variation, just be sure the kids have fun helping you decorate!

Cake

2 tablespoons butter, softened, or shortening, for greasing

All-purpose flour, for dusting

1 (15.9-ounce) box white cake mix

1 cup water

⅓ cup vegetable oil

3 eggs

1 teaspoon coconut extract

½ cup sweetened coconut flakes (optional)

1 cup canned cream of coconut

½ cup whole milk

Coconut Buttercream Frosting

½ cup (1 stick) butter, room temperature

2 cups powdered sugar

⅓ cup canned cream of coconut

2 teaspoons coconut extract

¾ cup sweetened coconut flakes

1. To make the cake, preheat the oven to 350°F. Prepare a 9 by 13-inch baking dish by spreading the softened butter evenly along the inside of the dish and then lightly dusting it with flour.

2. In a large bowl, stir together the cake mix, water, vegetable oil, eggs, and coconut extract. Beat with an electric hand mixer on medium speed until smooth and combined, about 2 minutes. Add the sweetened coconut flakes, if desired.

3. Pour the batter into the prepared baking dish and bake until golden brown, 30 to 35 minutes. Check for doneness by inserting a toothpick into the center of the cake. If it comes out clean, it's done. If it's not done, return it to the oven and bake for 2 to 3 minutes more. Remove the cake from the oven, place it on a cooling rack, and allow to cool for 20 minutes.

continued

Coconut Cake, continued

4 Poke holes in the cake with a fork or toothpick. In a small bowl, whisk together the cream of coconut and the milk until blended. Spoon the mixture over the warm cake, then allow it to cool completely.

5 When the cake has cooled, prepare the frosting. In a medium bowl and using the hand mixer, beat the butter on medium speed until creamy and fluffy, about 2 minutes. Continue beating and gradually add the powdered sugar, followed by the cream of coconut and coconut extract. Beat until well combined.

6 Frost the top of the cake and sprinkle it with sweetened coconut flakes. Refrigerate for at least 1 hour until you're ready to cut and serve.

side note

If you want to make cupcakes, a box of Dolly Parton's Favorite Coconut Flavored Cake Mix from Duncan Hines makes 24 cupcakes. Ice with Dolly Parton's Creamy Buttercream Frosting. We like to top them with coconut flakes and jelly beans . . . or you can let the kids in your family decorate them as they please!

May

Mother's Day — A Mother's Touch

Mother's Day—A Mother's Touch

We have one goal in mind with our Mother's Day meal—to celebrate your mom.

These dishes are meant to be made *for* Mom, not by her. Mothers love the simple act of you making the time—and the effort—to do something just for them. Even when we were young, we made sure Mother's Day was a special day for our mama. We realize now it was an early example of how food and family always go together.

Our mama taught us so much—all about life, of course, and especially about food. She's the reason we know how to cook, the reason we enjoy trying new things and creating new recipes, the reason we want people to feel welcome in our homes and have food for them to enjoy while there. She's been gone many years now, but we know she lives on in places like this book. Mama wasn't one to write down recipes, but she showed us how to make many dishes that you'll find on our tables. Often, they're created using one of her many skillets, treasured items we're lucky to have in our kitchens.

Mama would like this meal. It includes foods she made often and others we know she'd enjoy. We hope the "mom" in your life appreciates the time you put into making these dishes for her.

Mother's Day Mimosa

prep time: 5 minutes
makes 8 servings

Did Mama drink Champagne? We never knew Mama to drink, but she'd taste something new, just like us. We're a lot like her. She took a sip once at Rachel's house. It wasn't really a mimosa—more like orange juice with a whisper of Champagne on top, but she gave it a try! All our sisters enjoyed these that day, also. And why not—every mom deserves a little "sparkle" on Mother's Day.

— Dolly & Rachel

1 (750 ml) bottle Champagne, chilled

2 (11.5-ounce) bottles of orange juice

Pour the Champagne into eight flutes until each is half full. Top with orange juice. Cheers!

Opening Act: Watermelon Fruit Salad

prep time: 30 minutes plus chilling
makes 6 to 8 servings

This dish is pretty, colorful, and bright—much like our mama and everything that comes to mind when we think about spring. This recipe is meant to be made the morning of to ensure all the elements are as fresh as possible.

Fruit Salad

1 ripe seedless watermelon

1 ripe cantaloupe

1 ripe honeydew melon

2 cups hulled and halved strawberries

2 cups halved seedless green grapes

Champagne Dressing

¼ cup honey

¼ cup orange juice

¼ cup Champagne or sparkling white wine

1 teaspoon fresh lime zest

1 teaspoon fresh orange zest

3 tablespoons fresh lime juice

¼ cup minced fresh mint

1 Cut the watermelon in half lengthwise. Using a melon baller, scoop the watermelon into small rounds from both sides and place the rounds in a medium bowl. You will need 3 cups. Reserve the remaining watermelon for another use.

2 Cut the cantaloupe in half lengthwise and scoop out the seeds. Again using a melon baller, scoop out the cantaloupe into small rounds and place them in a separate medium bowl, and discard the rind. Repeat this process with the honeydew melon, placing the rounds in a third medium bowl.

3 Place each type of melon, the strawberries, and grapes in separate airtight containers (or resealable plastic bags) and refrigerate until chilled. Placing the fruit in separate containers keeps it fresh longer.

4 To make the dressing, in a medium bowl, whisk together the honey, orange juice, Champagne, lime zest, orange zest, and lime juice. Put the dressing in a small container and chill in the refrigerator. This can be done in advance to save time.

5 To serve, drain any juice from the melon containers and combine all the fruits in a large serving bowl. Sprinkle the mint over the fruit. Divide the fruit into individual servings, then drizzle each serving with some of the Champagne dressing.

> *side note* | Adding dressing to each portion—not the entire bowl—helps any leftover fruit keep longer.

Fried Chicken and Gravy

prep time: 15 minutes plus marinating time • cook time: 25 minutes
makes 4 to 6 servings

My kids and husband have always loved this particular recipe. Dolly, too. It takes more than one whole chicken to feed them all, though! For ease—and the best taste—marinate your chicken the night before. Doing so overnight gives the chicken the best flavor. Gravy can be intimidating—it just takes a little more time. Our mom made gravy every morning. It makes me appreciate her even more. Thanks, Mom.

— Rachel

Chicken

1 whole chicken, cut into 8 pieces

1½ teaspoons sea salt

1 teaspoon pepper

2 sprigs thyme

1 sprig rosemary

4 cups whole buttermilk, well shaken

2 eggs

2 tablespoons minced onion

3 garlic cloves, minced

1 tablespoon Tabasco sauce

½ cup shortening, plus more as needed

Breading

2 cups all-purpose flour

1 cup cornstarch

1 teaspoon salt

1 sprig thyme

1 sprig rosemary

Gravy

¼ cup chicken fat from skillet

¼ cup all-purpose flour

2 cups whole milk, room temperature

Salt and pepper

1 Marinate the chicken overnight for the best results. First, rinse the chicken pieces under cold water and pat thoroughly dry. Place the chicken in a large glass bowl. Sprinkle with the sea salt, pepper, and the leaves from the herb sprigs, which are easily stripped off by running your fingers down the stems.

2 In a medium bowl, combine the buttermilk, eggs, onion, garlic, and Tabasco and pour it over the chicken pieces. Cover and refrigerate the chicken overnight to marinate and tenderize the meat. You can also put the chicken and your marinade in a sealed plastic bag (inside a bowl in case there are any leaks). Feel free to move the chicken around in the marinade at some point while it marinates.

3 When you are ready to cook the chicken, remove it from the refrigerator. Place a wire rack inside a rimmed baking sheet. Line a second baking sheet with paper towels.

4 To make the breading, in a pie plate, whisk together the flour, cornstarch, and salt. Strip the leaves from the herb sprigs—no more than a teaspoon of each—by running your fingers down the stems, then add the leaves to the dry ingredients.

continued

Fried Chicken and Gravy, continued

5 Remove the chicken from the marinade, allowing any excess to drip back into the bowl or bag. Coat the chicken pieces thoroughly in the flour mixture. Place each piece on the prepared wire rack and let sit for 10 minutes. Discard the marinade once all the chicken has been removed. Also discard the flour mixture once breading is complete.

6 Preheat the oven to the lowest possible temperature setting.

7 Heat the shortening in a large cast-iron skillet over medium-high heat until a drop of water or a pinch of flour sizzles or dances on the top. Reduce the heat to medium and place the chicken pieces, skin-side down, into the skillet. Fry until golden brown, about 15 minutes. Rotate and fry the other side until golden brown and the chicken reaches an internal temperature of 165°F, another 10 minutes. Using tongs or a spider strainer, transfer the chicken to the paper towel–lined baking sheet. Chicken pieces can be fried in batches if they don't all fit easily in the skillet.

8 If you're frying in batches, add shortening (if needed) to the skillet and repeat with the remaining chicken pieces. Place the baking sheet in the warm oven until ready to serve.

9 To make the gravy, pour off all but ¼ cup of the fat from the skillet, leaving the darkened and crispy bits in the pan. Add the flour and whisk over low heat until the flour turns a nice golden brown and makes a roux, 2 to 4 minutes. This is the key to a rich, smooth gravy. Whisk in the milk, stirring constantly until combined. Allow the gravy to simmer until it thickens and nicely coats the back of a spoon. Season to taste with salt and pepper. Serve the chicken with gravy on the side.

side note

To make the gravy recipe separately and serve with another main dish, substitute ¼ cup shortening or bacon grease for the chicken fat.

Angel Biscuits

prep time: 15 minutes plus 2 hours chilling • cook time: 20 minutes
makes 30 biscuits

I'm not sure where the name "angel biscuits" came from—I've heard a lot of people use the phrase. I can't profess to knowing the origin of the biscuits, either. All I know is I've been making them forever and they're so good they must be from heaven. One thing I truly love about these is that you can bake what you need. You can make half of the dough (about 15 biscuits) in a 12-inch buttered skillet or make it all at once using a large parchment paper–lined baking sheet!

— Rachel

½ cup very warm water (about 110°F)

4½ teaspoons active dry yeast (2 packages)

1 teaspoon plus 3 tablespoons sugar

5 cups all-purpose flour (we like White Lily brand for this), plus more for dusting

1 tablespoon baking powder

2 teaspoons salt

1 teaspoon baking soda

½ cup (1 stick) cold butter, cubed

½ cup shortening, chilled

2 cups full-fat buttermilk, well shaken, room temperature

¼ cup (4 tablespoons) melted butter, for greasing and for brushing when done

1. In a small bowl, stir together the warm water, yeast, and 1 teaspoon of the sugar until the yeast and sugar are dissolved. Allow the mixture to sit for about 5 minutes. The yeast should be foamy or bubbly, meaning it's activated. If not, then your yeast may be bad. If this happens, discard and repeat the process with fresh yeast.
2. In a large bowl, combine the flour, baking powder, salt, baking soda, and remaining 3 tablespoons sugar. Cut the cold butter and shortening into the flour mixture using a pastry cutter until you get a crumbly consistency. Add the yeast mixture and buttermilk. Using a spatula or wooden spoon, stir the dough until the flour mixture is incorporated and the dry ingredients are thoroughly moistened.
3. Cover the bowl with plastic wrap and chill in the refrigerator for at least 2 hours (up to 3 days).
4. When ready to bake the biscuits, preheat the oven to 400°F. If using a 12-inch cast-iron skillet, grease the skillet with 2 tablespoons of the melted butter. If using a baking sheet, line it with parchment paper.

continued

Angel Biscuits, continued

5 Remove the dough from the refrigerator. Place the dough on a floured work surface and with floured hands, fold the dough in gently on all corners. Gather the edges of the dough with your fingertips and bring them toward the center. Remember, these are angel biscuits, *so handle them gently!* Turn the dough over and repeat.

6 Gently pat out the dough to about a 1-inch thickness. Use a 2½-inch biscuit cutter to cut out the biscuits. Transfer to the prepared skillet (you'll be able to fit about 15 in a 12-inch skillet; a 9-inch skillet is pictured) or arrange them, barely touching each other, on the prepared baking sheet. Any leftover biscuit dough can be kept in the refrigerator for up to 3 days so you can enjoy another batch with half the effort!

7 Bake for 15 to 20 minutes or until golden brown. Remove from the oven and brush the tops with the remaining melted butter.

8 Allow the biscuits to cool in the skillet or on the baking sheet for 5 minutes before serving in a napkin-lined basket or bowl.

Country Potato Salad

prep time: 25 minutes plus 1 hour chilling time
cook time: 18 minutes (not including hard-boiling the eggs)
makes 6 to 8 servings

We love potato salad. We have some real experts in our family—people who have their own special recipes. This is ours. It may have evolved over time, but once we reached this combination of ingredients, we both agreed—*this is it!* To us, it's one of the best things ever, whether it's for Mother's Day or Easter or any occasion.

- 5 pounds russet potatoes
- 1 teaspoon salt
- 1 cup mayonnaise
- ¼ cup heavy cream
- ¼ cup Dijon mustard
- 2 tablespoons white vinegar
- 6 hard-boiled eggs, peeled and quartered (see Side Note)
- 2 celery stalks, finely chopped
- ½ medium onion, finely chopped
- Finely chopped fresh dill, for garnish

1 Peel and cut the potatoes into ¾-inch pieces, place them in a colander, and rinse under cold water. Place them in a pot and cover with water. Add the salt and bring to a boil over high heat. Partially cover the pot, leaving an opening for steam to escape. Allow the potatoes to boil until fork-tender, about 18 minutes. Drain in the colander and allow to cool.

2 In a medium bowl, mix together the mayonnaise, heavy cream, mustard, and vinegar until thoroughly combined.

3 Place the potatoes, eggs, celery, and onion in a large bowl. Add the dressing and combine gently to evenly coat all the ingredients. Garnish with chopped dill. Cover and chill in the refrigerator for at least 1 hour or overnight before serving.

side note

To make hard-boiled eggs, refer to our Dressed Eggs recipe (page 74) and quarter the eggs. The eggs can also be hard-boiled 4 to 5 days in advance and stored in the refrigerator until you're ready to assemble the potato salad.

Oven-Roasted Broccoli

prep time: 10 minutes • cook time: 15 minutes
makes 6 servings

The way we grew up, some people would say we overcooked a lot of vegetables by simply boiling them, which, of course, could make them soft. And some people would be right. The first time we heard about roasting broccoli in the oven, we just couldn't imagine that. But it's wonderful! We didn't think about it when we were growing up, but there are so many things you can do with vegetables, and this is a perfect—and simple—example.

— Dolly & Rachel

4 cups broccoli florets, or 1 large head broccoli cut into bite-size pieces

¼ cup extra-virgin olive oil

1 garlic clove, minced

1 teaspoon salt

1 Preheat the oven to 400°F.

2 Place the broccoli in a large bowl. Add the olive oil, garlic, and salt and toss until well combined. Place the mixture on a rimmed baking sheet, spreading it out into a single layer so the broccoli cooks evenly. Bake until crisp-tender, 12 to 15 minutes. Serve warm.

side note | Several people in our family love to have chopped cooked bacon on top of this. But, of course, we do love our bacon!

Encore: Fresh Orange Cake

prep time: 25 minutes plus cooling time • cook time: 35 minutes
makes 10 servings

Growing up, something like this cake was a big deal. When we were little we loved what we called a stack pie, but we now know these as layer cakes. Mama made them sometimes, but we had one aunt on our mom's side who was known for her stack pies. They'd bake cakes and put a layer of applesauce or some other fruit in between. This is an old recipe—the orange juice and zest give it a surprise taste. And the glaze—not to mention the marshmallows—just makes it complete.

—Dolly & Rachel

Cake

½ cup shortening, plus more for greasing

2¼ cups cake flour, plus more for dusting

1 tablespoon baking powder

1 teaspoon salt

½ cup granulated sugar

2 eggs

½ cup whole milk

½ cup fresh orange juice

1 teaspoon fresh orange zest

1 cup miniature marshmallows

Orange Glaze

3 tablespoons butter, room temperature

1 tablespoon fresh orange zest

½ teaspoon salt

2 cups sifted powdered sugar

½ cup fresh orange juice

1 To make the cake, preheat the oven to 350°F and arrange a rack in the center. Grease one 8-inch round cake pan (for the top layer) and one 8-inch springform pan (for the bottom layer) with shortening and lightly dust each with flour.

2 Over a large bowl, sift together the cake flour, baking powder, and salt. Set aside.

3 In a large bowl and using an electric hand mixer, or in a stand mixer fitted with the paddle attachment, beat the shortening on medium speed while gradually adding the granulated sugar. Beat until light and fluffy, about 2 minutes. Add the eggs, one at a time, beating well after each addition. Add the sifted flour mixture and continue to beat until thoroughly combined and the batter is smooth.

4 Continue mixing, adding the milk, orange juice, and orange zest. Mix well until the batter is smooth, another 1 to 2 minutes. Divide the batter evenly between the prepared pans. Bake on the center rack until golden brown, about 35 minutes. Test by inserting a wooden toothpick into the center of the cake; if the toothpick

continued

Fresh Orange Cake, continued

comes out clean, the cake is done. If it's not done, return the cake to the oven and bake an additional 2 to 3 minutes.

5 Place the pans on a cooling rack. After 5 to 10 minutes, gently flip the 8-inch cake pan (top layer) and return the cake to the rack to cool. Leave the 8-inch springform cake (bottom layer) in its pan, but allow it to cool for 10 minutes.

6 Meanwhile, turn the broiler to high.

7 Arrange the marshmallows evenly on top of the bottom cake layer (still in the springform pan) and place it under the broiler until the marshmallows are soft and lightly browned, 1 to 2 minutes. Do not walk away from the oven—they will brown *very* quickly! Remove the pan and allow the cake to cool completely.

8 To make the orange glaze, in a large bowl and using the hand mixer or the stand mixer fitted with the paddle attachment, beat the butter on medium speed until light and fluffy, a minute or so. Add the orange zest and salt and mix to combine. Add half of the powdered sugar and half of the orange juice and continue to blend until thoroughly combined. Add the remaining powdered sugar and orange juice and continue blending until the glaze is smooth and thin enough to spoon over the cake.

9 Remove the bottom cake layer from the springform pan and transfer it to a cake plate. Spoon about half of the orange glaze over the toasted marshmallows. The glaze should run down the sides of cake. Top with the second cake layer (rounded top facing up) and finish by spooning the remaining orange glaze over the top. Slice and serve.

June

Father's Day—Firing Up the Grill

Father's Day—Firing Up the Grill

Warm weather brings lots of things—fruit starts to ripen on vines and bushes, vegetables are growing in the garden. The change in seasons also brings the opportunity to step outside (as much as we both love our kitchens) and to fire up the grill.

We love cooking out. And once we start, we aren't likely to stop until fall settles in. It's the ideal setting to enjoy time with family and friends—being outdoors means plenty of room for kids to run around, no limitations on how many people you can bring together, and more enjoyment for everyone, including us.

In our family, the fact that Father's Day arrives just as things are heating up provides a perfect reason to gather outdoors. With this menu, Dad can enjoy a cold drink and appetizer, and everyone can choose from chicken or steak specially grilled for the occasion, along with a summery salad. We like to finish the day with what may be the ultimate Southern dessert—one our daddy sure loved. There's nothing like our Mama's Banana Pudding.

Beer Bucket

prep time: 5 minutes

Who doesn't love a good cold beer? My husband and I do! Especially with some snacks before enjoying a summer dinner. Some of his favorites are Stella Artois, Miller Lite, and Modelo. A beer bucket allows you to create a variety of your own to please everyone!

Ice

Assorted favorite beers

Find yourself a good 8-gallon bucket. If you can't find a metal one, you can usually find plastic buckets with handles someplace like Party City or the local dollar store. Fill the bucket with ice and an assortment of your favorite beers.

STELLA ARTOIS
Lite
FINE PILSNER
Coors
Banquet
Modelo
Miller
HIGH LIFE
PREMIUM LAGER BEER
CERVEZA
Modelo
1925
Especial

Opening Act: Beef Queso

prep time: 10 minutes • cook time: 15 minutes
makes 6 to 8 servings

The dads and boys in our family just love this. And you can do it all in a single pan. Let's face it—it's meat, it's robust, and it's in snack form so you don't even have to cut it. It doesn't get any easier than that, from start to finish!

—Dolly & Rachel

- 2 teaspoons canola oil
- 1 pound ground beef
- ½ cup chopped onion
- ½ teaspoon salt
- ½ teaspoon pepper
- 1 teaspoon chili powder
- ½ teaspoon ground cumin
- ½ teaspoon dried oregano
- ¼ teaspoon red pepper flakes
- ½ cup petite diced tomatoes
- 1 (4-ounce) can chopped green chiles, drained
- ¼ cup salsa verde
- 1 cup cubed Velveeta
- ½ cup shredded Monterey Jack cheese
- 2 tablespoons finely chopped jalapeños, ribs and seeds removed if desired
- ¼ cup chopped fresh cilantro
- Tortilla chips, for serving

1. Heat the oil in an 8- to 10-inch cast-iron skillet over medium-high heat. Add the ground beef, onion, salt, and pepper. Cook, stirring to break up the meat, until the meat is no longer pink, 7 to 9 minutes. Remove the pan from the heat. Spoon off any excess fat if necessary.
2. Return the pan to medium heat and add the chili powder, cumin, oregano, and red pepper flakes. Stir until the meat is nicely coated in the spices. Add the tomatoes, green chiles, and salsa verde and stir until well combined.
3. Add the cheeses, stirring until they have thoroughly melted, 3 to 4 minutes. Stir in the jalapeño and cilantro. Taste for seasoning, adding more if needed. Transfer the queso to a serving bowl and serve warm with tortilla chips.

side notes

This dip can also be kept warm in a small slow cooker.

—Dolly

I love to sprinkle Tajín Clásico seasoning on my tortilla chips before serving. Not only is it pretty, it's delicious!

—Rachel

June

Grilled Chicken with Zesty Marinade

prep time: 15 minutes plus marinating • cook time: 8 minutes
makes 6 to 8 servings

I'm not as patient as Rachel is in the kitchen—I don't always want to take the time she does. But a nice marinade doesn't take long to make, and it does all the work! The marinade can really make the dish, too, whether it's vegetables or meats. This one gives the chicken outstanding flavor.

—Dolly

4 garlic cloves, minced

1 small onion, finely chopped

½ cup chopped fresh cilantro

½ cup extra-virgin olive oil

¼ cup fresh lime juice

1½ teaspoons paprika

1 teaspoon ground cumin

1 teaspoon minced fresh parsley

½ teaspoon salt

½ teaspoon red pepper flakes

3 boneless, skinless chicken breasts

1 medium onion, unpeeled

1 In a small bowl, stir together the garlic, chopped onion, cilantro, olive oil, lime juice, paprika, cumin, parsley, salt, and red pepper flakes until mixed thoroughly. Pour the marinade into a resealable plastic bag.

2 Rinse the chicken under cold water and pat thoroughly dry. Cut the breasts in half lengthwise. Add the chicken to the marinade, place the bag inside a bowl in case there are any leaks, and refrigerate for at least 1 hour or up to 3 hours. Feel free to turn the bag at least once while it marinates.

3 Remove the chicken from the refrigerator. Preheat the grill to high until the temperature reaches at least 500°F. Slice the whole onion in half, top to root (no need to remove the skin), skewer one half with a long grilling fork, and rub the cut side of the onion over the grill grates. (Reserve the remaining half onion for another use.) The heat will activate the onion's natural juices to remove any bits of charred food or debris and season the grill.

4 Lower the grill heat to medium. Remove the chicken from the marinade, discarding the marinade, and grill until the internal temperature reaches 165°F, 3 to 4 minutes per side. Remove from the heat and serve.

side note

If you have a grill with dual-side temperature control, you can cook the chicken on one side after cooking the T-bone steaks (see page 119) on the other.

T-bone Steak with Herb or Blue Cheese Butter

prep time: 15 minutes plus chilling and resting time • cook time: 10 minutes
makes 6 servings

We enjoy grilling, and when it comes to steak, you just have to have a pat of butter on it when it's finished. It does so much to enhance the taste. Having the herb butter and blue cheese butter ready and waiting in the fridge just makes something simple all that more special. Of course, we love butter, so we don't limit ourselves or our guests to a single pat—we make it a dollop.

— Dolly & Rachel

Blue Cheese Butter

½ cup (1 stick) salted butter, room temperature

¼ cup blue cheese, crumbled

Herb Butter

½ cup (1 stick) salted butter, room temperature

1 garlic clove, minced

1½ teaspoons chopped fresh rosemary or thyme

1½ teaspoons chopped fresh parsley

1½ teaspoons chopped fresh tarragon

¼ teaspoon salt

Steak

6 T-bone steaks

6 tablespoons extra-virgin olive oil

A generous amount of salt and pepper

Garlic powder

1 medium onion, unpeeled

1 To make the blue cheese butter, in a small bowl and using a fork, mash together the butter and blue cheese until combined. Using a melon baller, scoop four decorative rounds onto a small plate. Cover with plastic wrap and chill in the refrigerator until needed.

2 To make the herb butter, in a small bowl and using a fork, mash together the butter, garlic, rosemary, parsley, tarragon, and salt until combined. Using a melon baller, scoop four decorative rounds onto a small plate. Cover with plastic wrap and chill in the refrigerator until needed.

3 To prepare the steaks, remove them from refrigerator. Brush both sides of each steak with olive oil and season both sides very well with salt and pepper, as well as garlic powder to taste. Cover the steaks and let rest at room temperature for 30 minutes.

4 When you're ready to cook, preheat the grill to high until the temperature reaches at least 500°F. Slice the onion in half, top to root (no need to remove the skin), skewer one half with a long grilling fork, and rub the cut side of the onion over the grill grates.

continued

T-bone Steak with Herb or Blue Cheese Butter, continued

(Reserve the remaining half onion for another use.) The heat will activate the onion's natural juices to remove any bits of charred food or debris and season the grill.

5 Place the steaks on the grill and cook for 3 to 4 minutes per side (see our guide below). Remove the steaks from the grill. Place one round of flavored butter on each steak. Tent with foil and let rest for 10 minutes before serving.

Here's how to know when to remove the steaks from the grill:

Rare: Internal temperature will be 120° to 130°F

Medium rare: Internal temperature will be 130° to 140°F

Medium: Internal temperature will be 140° to 150°F

Well done: Burn it 😉

side note

If you have a grill with dual-side temperature control, you can cook the steaks on one side and the Grilled Chicken with Zesty Marinade (page 116) on the other.

Broccoli Salad

prep time: 15 minutes plus 1 hour chilling time
makes 6 to 8 servings

June

Salads are always good. I'm big on them, especially in the summer. My husband, Carl, likes salads year-round, and I can do a good salad whether it's using all sorts of vegetables or just one. There's nothing better than a summer garden salad, and this is a great one. And it's even better if you can make it the day before, so all the tastes and flavors can combine. Just give it a good stir before serving.

— Dolly

Dressing

1 cup mayonnaise

2 tablespoons apple cider vinegar

3 tablespoons powdered sugar

1 teaspoon salt

1 teaspoon pepper

Salad

8 cups broccoli florets, or 2 large heads broccoli cut into bite-size pieces

1 medium sweet onion, chopped

½ cup raisins

½ cup coarsely chopped raw pecans

6 slices (about ½ pound) bacon, cooked and chopped

1 To make the dressing, in a medium bowl, whisk together the mayonnaise, vinegar, powdered sugar, salt, and pepper and set aside.

2 To make the salad, in a large bowl, combine the broccoli, onion, raisins, pecans, and bacon. Drizzle with half of the dressing, stirring until well combined. Add the remaining dressing and mix thoroughly. Cover and refrigerate at least 1 hour or overnight.

side note | Any leftover broccoli salad can be stored in the refrigerator for up to 4 days.

Encore: Mama's Banana Pudding

prep time: 25 minutes plus cooling time • cook time: 15 minutes
makes enough to serve a house full of hungry kids (and adults, too!)

There are so many versions of banana pudding—or puddin', as we call it. This one allows you to make it from scratch like we do and always have, just like our mama and our grandmas and our aunts used to. If you don't have time for that, Rachel's "quick and easy" option, which follows, is a great summer dessert. No matter what you do, just be sure to make enough! After putting in the effort, you don't want to be the one to go, "Where's the banana pudding? I missed it!"

— Dolly & Rachel

Pudding

1 cup sugar

½ cup all-purpose flour

⅛ teaspoon salt

6 cups whole milk

6 egg yolks (set aside the egg whites for the meringue topping)

3 whole eggs

½ cup (1 stick) butter

2 teaspoons vanilla extract

9 ripe bananas

2 (12-ounce) boxes vanilla wafers

Meringue

6 egg whites, room temperature (reserved from pudding recipe)

1 tablespoon sugar

¼ teaspoon cream of tartar

1 teaspoon vanilla extract

1 To make the pudding, in a large bowl, combine the sugar, flour, and salt. Add the milk, egg yolks, and whole eggs. Whisk until well combined to create a thick custard mixture.

2 In a large saucepan, melt the butter over medium heat. Pour the custard mixture into the saucepan, turn down the heat to medium-low, and whisk slowly to combine. Stir constantly until the custard has thickened and coats the back of a spoon nicely. Remove the custard from the heat and stir in the vanilla. Cover and allow the custard to cool to room temperature. It will continue to thicken as it cools.

3 Peel and slice the bananas into ¼-inch-thick rounds. Line a 9 by 13-inch casserole dish with the vanilla wafers, placing them on the bottom and up the sides. Then layer the banana slices the same way. Pour the cooled custard mixture over the bananas and wafers, smoothing the top with a knife or spatula.

4 To make the meringue, in a large bowl, using an electric hand mixer, or in a stand mixer fitted with the whisk attachment, beat the egg whites, sugar, cream of tartar,

continued

Mama's Banana Pudding, continued

and vanilla on high speed until stiff peaks form. Spoon this mixture over the top of the custard, covering it completely.

5. Adjust the top oven rack so that it's a couple of inches away from the broiler and turn the broiler to high. Quickly brown the meringue, about 2 minutes. This happens very quickly, so don't walk away or it may burn!
6. Remove the dish from the oven, allow the meringue to cool, and serve. The banana pudding will keep in the refrigerator, covered, up to 4 days.

Quick and Easy Banana Pudding

makes 6 to 8 servings

If you don't want to make a custard, this alternative is a family favorite in our homes! It's easy to make and even easier for us to eat. It's always the first thing to go at our family gatherings . . . just like the traditional version!

- 2 small (3.4-ounce) boxes vanilla Jell-O instant pudding and pie filling
- 4 cups cold whole milk
- 1 (14-ounce) can Eagle brand sweetened condensed milk
- 1 (8-ounce) container Cool Whip
- 1 (4-ounce) container sour cream
- 5 or 6 bananas
- 1 (12-ounce) box vanilla wafers

1. In a large bowl, use an electric hand mixer to combine the instant pudding and cold milk on medium speed until well incorporated. Add the condensed milk, Cool Whip, and sour cream and mix until incorporated. Cover with plastic wrap and set aside. The mixture will set up within 5 minutes.
2. While the pudding mixture thickens, peel and slice the bananas into ¼-inch-thick rounds.
3. Spoon approximately a quarter of the pudding mixture into the bottom of a glass trifle bowl and smooth it with a knife or spatula. Add a layer of bananas, using about a third of the slices. Add a layer of wafers, using about a third of them.
4. Repeat this process two more times, layering pudding, banana slices, and wafers into the trifle dish. Reserve a couple wafers and crumble them. End with a final layer of the remaining pudding and sprinkle the wafer crumbs on top.

July

Fourth of July ~ Celebration Cookout

Fourth of July—Celebration Cookout

Sweet tea . . . barbecue . . . corn on the cob . . . apple pie. Does any combination say "summertime" better? Add fireworks and the Fourth of July, and you have a Celebration Cookout.

It doesn't matter where you are—there's just nothing like the smell of outdoor cooking. We have a place on a lake, and in the summer it seems like everybody has a grill going either out by the water or on their boat. You can smell the food cooking, and it all just seems to go together.

Sometimes as kids we'd get to go to town on the Fourth of July, where we could get corn on the cob or ribs. It was all so good. Maybe that's why it just felt right to put barbecue ribs and grilled corn at the center of this celebration meal! But the fact of the matter is, this summertime menu is perfect no matter when or where you decide to make it—on the lake, at home, or for the Fourth.

Sweet Tea

prep time: 10 minutes plus 2 hours chilling time • cook time: 20 minutes
makes 1 gallon

Sweet tea is just so Southern. And so are we! So, true to form, here it is—not only for all the Southern girls and boys but for every*one* every*where*. It's perfect for summer no matter where you are—the lemons and fresh mint make it a wonderful, refreshing drink.

— Dolly & Rachel

16 cups water

5 family-size tea bags, or 6 regular-size tea bags

A pinch of baking soda

1 cup sugar, or to taste

Fresh lemon wedges, for serving

Fresh mint, for serving

1 Place 4 cups of the water in a medium saucepan and bring to a boil. Remove from the heat. Tie together the strings of the tea bags and place them into the saucepan with the string tabs over the edge of the pot. Cover and steep for 15 minutes.

2 Remove the lid, use a spoon to gently press the tea bags to extract as much tea as possible, and discard the tea bags. Stir in the baking soda. Add the sugar and stir until dissolved. Transfer the tea to a large serving pitcher and stir in the remaining 12 cups water. Refrigerate for at least 2 hours.

3 Serve over ice with lemon wedges and mint.

22
20
18
16
Microwave Safe
700
600
500

Opening Act: Hot Wing Dip with Celery Sticks

prep time: 10 minutes • cook time: 5 minutes
makes 6 to 8 servings

This packs a little heat, and we like that. So things are about to get hot! You really have to watch who's in control of the hot sauce on this one! But you can adjust the recipe to your liking. This buffalo wing–inspired dip delivers, no matter how much heat you put into it.

— Dolly & Rachel

1 rotisserie chicken, meat shredded and skin discarded

2 (8-ounce) blocks cream cheese

1 (6-ounce) bottle Texas Pete hot sauce

1 cup blue cheese dressing

2 cups shredded cheddar cheese

2 to 3 tablespoons blue cheese crumbles, for garnish

1 bunch celery, washed and cut into 4-inch pieces, for serving

Club crackers, for serving

1 In a large saucepan, combine the chicken, cream cheese, hot sauce, blue cheese dressing, and cheddar cheese. Cook over medium heat, stirring frequently, until all the cheeses are smooth and melted, about 5 minutes.

2 Transfer the dip to a serving bowl and garnish with blue cheese crumbles. Serve with celery and crackers.

side note | If you want to keep this warm, place the dip in a slow cooker on low.

Grilled Corn with Spicy Mayo

prep time: 15 minutes plus soaking time • cook time: 15 minutes
makes 6 to 8 servings

You may be familiar with this or know it as "street corn"—that's how we discovered it. If we're going to be outside enjoying the summer weather, we often soak the corn in a small cooler near the grill. That way we can easily grab it when the time comes to cook the corn after other items have come off the grill—and spend that much more time with family and friends.

— Dolly & Rachel

Corn

6 to 8 ears of sweet corn (1 per person)

1 lime, cut into 6 to 8 wedges, for serving

Salt and pepper to taste

Spicy Mayo

1 cup mayonnaise

½ cup grated Parmesan cheese, plus more for serving

2 tablespoons minced fresh cilantro

2 teaspoons fresh lime juice

½ teaspoon chili powder, plus more for serving

Special Equipment

Kitchen twine

1 To prepare the corn, pull the husks back from the corn cobs, keeping them attached while removing the silks. Re-cover the cobs with their husks and twist them at the top to secure. Tie the tops with 10-inch lengths of kitchen twine. Place the corn in a large pot of cold water and let soak 1 hour.

2 Meanwhile, prepare the spicy mayo. In a small bowl, mix together the mayonnaise, Parmesan, cilantro, lime juice, and chili powder until thoroughly combined.

3 Preheat a grill to medium-high (350° to 400°F). Place the corn on the grill and cook, turning occasionally, until the husks are charred and the corn has steamed, 12 to 15 minutes. Remove the corn from the grill and allow it to cool enough to handle.

4 Shuck the corn. Using a basting brush or a spoon, apply the spicy mayo mixture to the corn. Sprinkle with additional Parmesan cheese and chili powder. Serve the corn with lime wedges, salt, and pepper.

side note You can make the spicy mayo while the corn soaks or prepare it in advance and refrigerate.

Layered Salad

prep time: 20 minutes plus 4 hours chilling
makes 8 to 10 servings

Presentation matters, and that's especially true here. You want people to see the layers, so make sure to use a nice glass bowl or a trifle bowl that you'd typically use for desserts to show off the layers. It's definitely best if you can make this ahead of time. All the tastes are enhanced as it sits. The creamy combination of three simple ingredients creates a dressing that complements every individual item in this salad. Wait until you taste them all together!

- 2 cups mayonnaise
- 1 cup sour cream
- ½ cup grated Parmesan cheese
- 2 teaspoons sugar
- ½ teaspoon salt, plus more to taste
- ½ teaspoon pepper, plus more to taste
- 8 ounces fresh spinach, washed, dried, and chopped
- ½ pound bacon (about 6 slices), cooked and crumbled
- 6 hard-boiled eggs (see page 74), peeled and chopped
- 1 medium head iceberg lettuce, washed, dried, cored, and chopped
- 1 medium red onion, chopped
- 10 ounces frozen peas
- 2 cups shredded cheddar cheese

1. In a small bowl, mix together the mayonnaise, sour cream, and Parmesan cheese. Set aside.
2. In another small bowl, combine the sugar, salt, and pepper. In a large glass serving bowl or trifle bowl, layer the spinach on the bottom. Sprinkle half of the sugar mixture over the spinach.
3. Sprinkle the spinach with the crumbled bacon and chopped egg. Layer on the iceberg lettuce and sprinkle with the remaining sugar mixture. Add a layer of chopped red onion, then the frozen peas. Spoon in the mayonnaise–sour cream mixture, smoothing the top to cover. Top evenly with the shredded cheddar, cover, and refrigerate at least 4 hours before serving.
4. To serve, use salad serving utensils to remove layered portions onto plates.

side note

We often make this the night before serving for convenience and better taste.

Barbecue Ribs

prep time: 15 minutes • cook time: 2 hours 5 minutes
makes 6 to 8 servings

We love ribs. And though it may be a surprise to see, pickling spices work sort of like a marinade—it's a wonderful thing. Using the spices when you precook the ribs makes the meat incredibly tender, and the ribs are already cooked through by the time they hit the grill. Putting them on the grill over a flame brings out even more of the flavor and adds some nice caramelization, too. And the spices work with either beef or pork!

Ribs

3 to 4 pounds beef or pork ribs

1 (1.5-ounce) container McCormick Pickling Spice (you should be able to find this in the spice or canning section of your local store)

Seasoning Blend

1 teaspoon garlic powder

1 teaspoon Cajun seasoning

1 teaspoon onion powder

1 teaspoon salt

1 teaspoon pepper

½ teaspoon sugar

Barbecue Sauce

1 cup store-bought barbecue sauce

½ cup sweet chili sauce (we like Mae Ploy)

¼ cup Worcestershire sauce

1. To prepare the ribs, cut them into portions small enough to fit into a large pot.
2. Add 8 cups of water and pickling spice to a large pot and bring to a boil over medium-high heat. Remove the pot from the heat, cover, and let steep for 10 minutes. Add the ribs; if needed, add more water until they are covered.
3. Return the pot to medium-high heat, uncovered. Bring to a boil, lower the heat to medium, cover, and continue cooking for 30 minutes. Turn the ribs in the water and continue cooking 30 minutes more.
4. Turn down the heat to low and simmer for another 30 minutes (1½ hours total). Low and slow is the way to cook ribs—either pork or beef—otherwise the meat won't be nice and tender.
5. Meanwhile, make the seasoning blend. In a small bowl, combine the garlic powder, Cajun seasoning, onion powder, salt, pepper, and sugar. Set aside.
6. Next, make the barbecue sauce. In a medium bowl, combine the barbecue sauce, chili sauce, and Worcestershire until smooth. Set aside.

continued

Barbecue Ribs, continued

7 Remove the ribs from the pot and place them on a serving plate or platter. Sprinkle with the seasoning blend, turning to coat both sides. Baste with the barbecue sauce on all sides.

8 Preheat the grill to medium-high heat. When it's ready, place the ribs on the grill and turn every 5 minutes, reapplying barbecue sauce each time, for a total of 15 minutes. The ribs will be nicely glazed with a slightly charred flavor.

Encore: Apple Pie with Crumb Topping

prep time: 30 minutes • cook time: 1 hour
makes 6 to 8 servings

There are people who might say there's nothing more American than apple pie, except maybe Dolly, and they'd probably be right. This recipe combines all the things we love about apple pie—the cinnamon, nutmeg, cloves, and of course the sugar—but it's also easy as pie to make, because the filling bakes with a simple crumb topping.

— 

Filling

¼ cup (½ stick) butter

7 or 8 Granny Smith or Honeycrisp apples, peeled, cored, and cut into wedges

⅔ cup sugar

1 teaspoon lemon juice

¼ teaspoon salt

½ teaspoon ground cinnamon

¼ teaspoon ground nutmeg

⅛ teaspoon ground cloves

1 tablespoon all-purpose flour

1 tablespoon cornstarch

Cooking spray, for greasing (if needed)

1 (9-inch) pie crust, store-bought or homemade (see page 32)

Crumb Topping

1 cup old-fashioned rolled oats

½ cup packed brown sugar

¼ cup sugar

½ teaspoon salt

½ teaspoon ground cinnamon

½ cup (1 stick) cold butter, sliced

1 Preheat the oven to 400°F.

2 To make the filling, in a large cast-iron skillet over medium-high heat, melt the butter. Add the apple wedges and cook for 2 minutes. Stir in the sugar, lemon juice, salt, cinnamon, nutmeg, and cloves. Continue cooking, stirring occasionally, for 10 minutes. Sprinkle the apples with the flour and cornstarch and cook until thickened, another 2 to 3 minutes. Transfer the apple mixture to a bowl and cool to room temperature.

3 If you're using a premade pie crust, take it out of the freezer and place in the refrigerator. If you're making your own crust, prepare a 9-inch pie plate with cooking spray, press the rolled-out

> *side note* | Put the filled pie plate on a baking sheet to catch any spillover while the pie bakes. You'll save time later when you don't have to clean your oven!

continued

Apple Pie with Crumb Topping, continued

crust into the plate, and crimp the edges with a fork or your fingers. Place the pie crust in the refrigerator while you make the crumb topping.

4 To make the crumb topping, in the bowl of a food processor fitted with the blade attachment, combine the rolled oats, both sugars, salt, and cinnamon. Pulse a few times to incorporate, then add the butter slices and pulse a few more times to create a coarse and crumbly consistency.

5 Remove the pie crust from the refrigerator. Add the cooled apple mixture to the crust, spreading it evenly, then sprinkle the crumb topping over the apples. Bake for 15 minutes. Lower the temperature to 350°F and continue baking until the crumbs are golden brown, about 30 minutes more.

6 Allow the pie to cool for 20 minutes, then slice and serve.

August

Summertime—Gone Fishin'

Summertime—Gone Fishin'

Every meal and every recipe has a reason and a purpose. The meal might reflect the season or a special occasion. Sometimes the purpose is simply to create a variety of dishes that all come together, complement each other, and leave everyone with a smile on their face.

This is a meal that does all that. These foods just go together! There's not necessarily any tradition behind this list (though there is behind some of the recipes), but when you make the dishes together, it becomes a perfect summer meal.

You don't need to spend all sorts of money on exotic ingredients or have a gourmet kitchen to make great—and good lookin'—food. Everything on the following pages reflects that. Nachos, fried fish, fritters, slaw, potato wedges—you can tell they all go together just by saying the words aloud. Cap the meal with strawberry shortcake and you've done it—created a complete meal whose simple purpose may be just to make everyone smile.

Opening Act: Nachos with Homemade Salsa

prep time: 20 minutes • cook time: 20 minutes
makes 6 to 8 servings

A friend of mine recently introduced me to Tajín Clásico, a Mexican spice blend, and it's a wonder. It has a little heat . . . a taste of lime . . . and you can find it with the other spices at the store. This homemade salsa is fresh, easy, delicious, and lasts for up to a week refrigerated in an airtight container.

— Rachel

Homemade Salsa (makes enough to fill one 32-ounce mason jar)

4 or 5 ripe medium tomatoes, cored and chopped

1 (14.5-ounce) can petite diced tomatoes, with juices

¼ cup onion, chopped

2 jalapeños, seeded and chopped

1½ cups chopped fresh cilantro

Juice of 2 limes (about ¼ cup)

1 teaspoon sugar

1 teaspoon salt

1 teaspoon pepper

1 teaspoon chili powder

½ teaspoon garlic powder

½ teaspoon ground cumin

Ground Beef Mixture

1 pound ground beef

1½ teaspoons salt

½ cup chopped sweet onion

2 ripe medium tomatoes, chopped

1 (4-ounce) can chopped green chiles

1½ teaspoons chili powder

½ teaspoon ground cumin

¼ teaspoon sugar

¾ cup plus 2 teaspoons salsa, homemade or store-bought

1 tablespoon cornstarch

To Assemble and Serve

1 (18-ounce) bag tortilla chips

3 cups shredded cheese blend

1 medium tomato, cored and chopped

4 green onions, chopped

2 to 3 tablespoons chopped fresh cilantro

Tajín Clásico seasoning

1 (8-ounce) container sour cream

1 lime, cut into wedges

1. To make the salsa, in the bowl of a food processor fitted with the blade attachment, combine the fresh tomatoes, canned tomatoes, onion, jalapeños, cilantro, lime juice, sugar, salt, pepper, chili powder, garlic powder, and cumin. Pulse until finely chopped, about four pulses.

2. To make the ground beef mixture, preheat the oven to 350°F. Place the ground beef in a large skillet, season with 1 teaspoon of the salt, and cook over medium-high heat until browned, 7 to 9 minutes.

3 Spoon off the excess fat from the meat. Stir in the sweet onion, tomatoes, and half of the green chiles. Add the chili powder, cumin, sugar, and remaining ½ teaspoon salt and stir to combine. Add ¾ cup of the salsa and bring to a simmer over medium-low heat.

4 In a small bowl, combine the cornstarch with the remaining 2 teaspoons salsa, mixing them together into a paste. Add the paste to the beef mixture and continue to cook until it thickens slightly, 4 to 5 minutes. Remove the skillet from the heat.

5 To assemble and serve, spread the tortilla chips out on a rimmed baking sheet. Spoon the ground beef mixture over the chips, then sprinkle with the shredded cheese. Bake until the cheese is bubbly, about 5 minutes.

6 Transfer the baked chips to a serving platter and garnish with the chopped tomato, green onions, and cilantro. Sprinkle with Tajín Clásico. Serve with a bowl of sour cream, lime wedges, and fresh homemade salsa.

side note

The salsa and the beef mixture can be made in advance and refrigerated until you're ready to cook and serve.

Fried Trout or Catfish

prep time: 10 minutes • cook time: 10 minutes
makes 6 to 8 servings

We grew up with fried fish. We'd go to the river with Daddy. He caught the fish, Mama fried them, and we ate them. Our Daddy was always scared that one of us was going to get a fishbone—he'd be sitting at the head of the table making sure there were none because he was not about to let that happen. By the time he had watched us all eat, he hadn't gotten to enjoy the fish when it was hot!

— Dolly & Rachel

Peanut oil or canola oil (enough to fill a deep fryer or Dutch oven halfway)

2 cups cornmeal mix

3 tablespoons Old Bay seasoning

2 teaspoons salt, plus more for seasoning

1 teaspoon pepper, plus more for seasoning

1 teaspoon garlic powder

1 teaspoon onion powder

6 trout or catfish fillets, rinsed in cold water and patted dry

1 In a deep fryer or a large Dutch oven and using a deep-fry thermometer, heat 2 to 3 inches of oil to 350°F. Line a rimmed baking sheet with paper towels.

2 In a pie plate or baking dish, mix together the cornmeal mix, Old Bay, salt, pepper, garlic powder, and onion powder.

3 Season both sides of the fish with salt and pepper. Dredge the fillets in the cornmeal mixture. Gently add them to the hot oil and deep-fry for 3 minutes, then turn and continue to fry until golden brown, 2 minutes more. You'll likely have to do this in batches so as not to crowd the pot. Remove the fried fish to the prepared baking sheet to drain. Serve hot.

Corn Fritters

prep time: 15 minutes • cook time: 15 minutes
makes 6 to 8 servings of multiple fritters

We grew up with corn—it was a staple. Not just sweet corn, but the corn we'd help Daddy pull in the fall, put in baskets, and shuck to take to the mill and have ground up for the winter. We've told the story for years that the doctor who rode in on horseback to deliver Dolly was paid with a sack of cornmeal that Daddy had ground. Corn means a lot to us for many, many reasons! And since it's so abundant in the summer, why not try something besides corn on the cob? Fresh corn, cornmeal, eggs, all fried in an electric skillet for more even cooking: how could it not be good?

—Dolly & Rachel

Peanut oil or canola oil, for frying
1⅔ cups cornmeal mix
1½ tablespoons sugar
1 teaspoon baking powder
1 teaspoon salt
1 teaspoon pepper
2 eggs
¾ cup whole buttermilk, well shaken
2 tablespoons butter, melted and cooled
2 cups fresh corn kernels (from about 3 ears of corn)

Special Equipment
Electric skillet

1 Set an electric skillet to 350°F. If using a cast-iron skillet, heat it over medium-high heat. Add enough of the oil to cover the bottom of the skillet, about ¼ cup. Line a plate with paper towels.

2 In a medium bowl, whisk together the cornmeal mix, sugar, baking powder, salt, and pepper until combined. In a separate bowl, whisk together the eggs, buttermilk, and butter.

3 Pour the liquid mixture into the dry ingredients and mix until combined. The batter will remain lumpy. Gently fold in the corn. With a medium-size cookie scoop or small measuring cup, scoop out a small portion of the batter and gently drop it into the hot oil, and continue scooping the batter to make more fritters. Do not overcrowd the skillet; we make 6 to 8 at one time. Allow the fritters to cook on the first side until golden brown, 2 to 4 minutes. Flip using a spatula and cook until golden brown on the other side and cooked through, 2 to 4 minutes more.

4 Remove the fritters from the hot oil and drain them on the prepared plate. Repeat with the remaining batter. Serve the fritters warm.

side note
To keep your fritters warm, place them on a small baking sheet in a preheated 175°F oven until all of them are done cooking.

Purple and White Slaw

prep time: 20 minutes plus 2 hours chilling
makes 6 to 8 servings

We had never seen a purple cabbage until we had grown up—the white cabbage Daddy grew was all we'd known. But purple cabbage makes a beautiful slaw . . . and using your own dressing makes it special. It takes just a little more time, and it's always worth it. Dolly loves slaw so much she almost always has one in her refrigerator!

— Dolly & Rachel

1 (1-pound) white cabbage, finely shredded

1 (1-pound) purple cabbage, finely shredded

2 carrots, peeled and shredded

2 celery stalks, washed and chopped

1 small onion, finely chopped

¾ cup mayonnaise

½ cup sour cream

2 tablespoons Dijon mustard

2 tablespoons apple cider vinegar

1 tablespoon sugar

2 teaspoons celery seeds

1 teaspoon celery salt

Salt and pepper to taste

In a large bowl, toss together the cabbages, carrots, celery, and onion, mixing thoroughly. In a small bowl, combine the mayonnaise, sour cream, mustard, vinegar, sugar, celery seeds, celery salt, and salt and pepper, stirring until well blended. Pour the dressing over the vegetables and toss to coat. Cover and chill at least 2 hours, allowing the vegetables to marinate, before serving.

side note | Using a food processor to shred and chop the vegetables is a huge time-saver!

Broiled Potato Wedges

prep time: 10 minutes • cook time: 40 minutes
makes 6 to 8 servings

In the summer, you don't necessarily want to be standing over the stove, and this recipe makes potatoes part of a meal without having to. And it's so easy to do—prepare the potatoes using oil and seasoning, and the oven does the rest. We garnish with a little parsley, but once you taste these, you may feel that a dollop of sour cream or other toppings you associate with a baked potato are a nice touch, too!

4 large russet potatoes, scrubbed

3 tablespoons extra-virgin olive oil

1 teaspoon salt

1 teaspoon pepper

1 teaspoon garlic powder

½ teaspoon onion powder

2 tablespoons minced fresh parsley, for garnish

1. Preheat the oven to 425°F.
2. Slice the potatoes in half lengthwise, then cut each half into four wedges. Rinse the potatoes in a colander until the water runs clear. Remove and pat them dry.
3. Place the wedges in a large bowl, drizzle with the olive oil, and sprinkle with the salt, pepper, garlic powder, and onion powder. Toss the potatoes until evenly coated.
4. Arrange the potato wedges on a baking sheet in a single layer for even baking. Roast until golden brown and tender, flipping the wedges halfway through, 35 to 40 minutes.
5. Garnish the potatoes with minced parsley and serve.

Encore: Strawberry Shortcake

prep time: 30 minutes plus 1 hour cooling • cook time: 30 minutes
makes 6 to 8 servings

In our childhood, when the time came every year, Daddy would take us down to a place called Tellico Plains, where there were fields of strawberries. We gathered up baskets of them to bring home, though of course we'd eat more than we picked. We loved strawberries then and still do now, so much so that Rachel created this recipe, which everyone loves. It's just a wonderful biscuit with a lot of sugar, a true shortcake. The glaze is an added touch that's pretty and sweet and makes this dessert very special.

— Dolly & Rachel

Shortcake

2½ cups all-purpose flour, plus more for dusting

¾ cup granulated sugar

1 teaspoon baking powder

½ teaspoon salt

½ cup (1 stick) cold butter, sliced, plus more for greasing

2 eggs, beaten

1 cup heavy cream, or ¾ cup whole milk

½ teaspoon vanilla extract

Strawberries

4 cups washed, hulled, and halved strawberries (if desired, reserve 3 of the prettiest small strawberries whole with stems for garnish)

1 teaspoon powdered sugar

Whipped Cream

1½ cups cold heavy cream

¼ cup powdered sugar

1 teaspoon vanilla extract

Glaze

¼ cup (½ stick) butter

1 cup powdered sugar

2 teaspoons whole milk

1 Preheat the oven to 350°F. Butter and flour an 8-inch round cake pan.

2 To make the shortcake, in a food processor fitted with the blade attachment, combine the flour, granulated sugar, baking powder, and salt and pulse until well mixed. Drop the sliced butter into the processor, a few pieces at a time, and pulse until the mixture is crumbly. Add the eggs, heavy cream, and vanilla and pulse again a few times until combined. Don't overprocess.

3 Turn the dough out onto a lightly floured surface and gently knead the dough four or five times.

continued

Strawberry Shortcake, continued

4 Gently pat the dough evenly into the prepared pan. Bake until lightly golden brown, about 30 minutes. Test by inserting a wooden toothpick into the center of the cake; if the toothpick comes out clean, the cake is done. If it's not done, return it to the oven and bake an additional 2 to 3 minutes.

5 Remove the shortcake from the oven and gently turn it out onto a cooling rack. Allow to cool completely, about 1 hour.

6 While the cake cools, place the halved strawberries in a bowl and sprinkle with the powdered sugar. Set aside.

7 To make the whipped cream, in a chilled medium bowl (see Side Note), combine the cream, powdered sugar, and vanilla. Using an electric hand mixer, blend on medium speed until well combined. Change the mixer speed to high and whip until soft peaks form.

8 To make the glaze, melt the butter in a small saucepan over medium heat. Stir in the powdered sugar and continue stirring until well combined. Add the milk, 1 teaspoon at a time, using just enough to thin the glaze to your desired consistency. It needs to be thin enough to drizzle over the shortcake with a spoon.

9 When the shortcake is cool, carefully cut it in half horizontally to make two layers. Place the bottom layer on a cake plate. Add a layer of whipped cream on top, using approximately half. Top with half of the prepared strawberries. Drizzle the glaze by the spoonful over the strawberries until it drips over the sides of the shortcake layer. Add the top cake layer and cover it with the remaining whipped cream and strawberries. If desired, partially slice each of the 3 reserved strawberries into three sections and fan them out on top.

10 If necessary, gently warm the glaze again to a thin, spoonable consistency. Be careful not to make it too hot or it'll melt the whipped cream! Drizzle the glaze by the spoonful over the sides and across the top. How much you use is up to you—you will have extra! (Treat yourself to a spoonful, if you want! Leftover glaze can be stored for a few days in the refrigerator.)

side note

I put a medium metal or glass bowl into the refrigerator to chill before whipping the cream. I find this helps keep the cream cold while preparing it.

—Rachel

CLUB

September

Something for Everyone—Road Happy

Something for Everyone—Road Happy

Food, travel, and the road go hand in hand—we discovered that a long time ago. When you're on the road, you're still surrounded by family—your touring family. You spend a lot of time together, and people become close.

Just like at home, that closeness happens around food. You want your road family to be happy. You want them to enjoy the experience. And shared meals help do that.

In the early days, we always had a little refrigerator on the bus and later a microwave, which we wore out. We also knew every good restaurant on every highway, whether it was a truck stop or a steak house. Sometimes we knew routes by the food as much as by the cities we were headed to!

Over the years, when we could have catering on tour, we made sure it was good food, just like we would eat at home. After a rehearsal, there'd be a big supper before the show itself. The food often included the kinds of things we'd have made if we were in our own kitchens. Food brings people together—it always has and always will. That's true no matter where you are, whether far from home or gathered around your own table.

Dirt Road Martini

prep time: 5 minutes
makes 1 martini

Olives come to mind for just about everybody when they think of a martini, but why stop there? We like the taste that tea and pickled vegetables give this, Rachel's version of the classic drink. Giardiniera is a colorful combination of pickled carrots, cauliflower, celery, pickles, red bell peppers, and onions that make this martini especially good lookin'.

—Dolly & Rachel

2 ounces vodka

2 ounces unsweetened tea

1½ teaspoons brine from Mezzetta Italian Mix Giardiniera

Spanish Queen martini olives (pitted or stuffed)

Vegetable pieces from Mezzetta Italian Mix Giardiniera

Ice, for serving

Toothpick

1 In a mixing glass, combine the vodka, unsweetened tea, and brine. Stir well with a spoon.

2 Fill a lowball or rocks glass with ice. Pour the stirred martini mixture over the ice. Garnish with a toothpick skewer of olives and assorted giardiniera. Enjoy!

Opening Act: Shrimp with Cream Cheese, Capers, and Cocktail Sauce

prep time: 10 minutes
makes 6 to 8 servings

One weekend evening, we were having a little wine on what we call a "sister night" with our sibling Cassie. Dolly asked if there was anything to snack on, and Rachel said, "I'll be right back." And she returned with this all laid out, using things she already had on hand! You cannot go wrong with it, whether it's with a glass of wine or a special occasion when you have company over. We all loved it so much that we now keep these items handy all the time.

—Dolly & Rachel

Cocktail Sauce

½ cup chili sauce

2 tablespoons prepared horseradish, to taste

1 teaspoon lemon juice

½ teaspoon Worcestershire sauce

½ teaspoon hot sauce

To Serve

5 large shrimp per person, precooked and deveined, tail on (see Side Notes)

1 (8-ounce) block cream cheese

2 tablespoons drained capers

Assorted crackers

1 To make the cocktail sauce, in a small bowl, combine the chili sauce, horseradish, lemon juice, Worcestershire, and hot sauce. If not serving immediately, cover and chill in the refrigerator.

2 To serve, put the shrimp on ice. Spread the cream cheese over a decorative plate. Pour the cocktail sauce over the top of the cream cheese and garnish it with capers. Serve with assorted party crackers.

side notes

This is something I often make as a quick and easy appetizer. It's perfect with the Dirt Road Martini (page 168) and also delicious with a crisp, cold Chardonnay!

You can rinse the shrimp after cooking with a lemon mixture. Combine ½ cup lemon juice, ½ cup water, and ½ teaspoon salt, mix well, and pour it over the cooked shrimp in a colander. Rinse the shrimp in cold water, drain well, and place them in a resealable plastic bag. Refrigerate until ready to use. We love the lemon taste!

—Rachel

Family Favorite Meatloaf

prep time: 25 minutes • cook time: 1 hour
makes 6 to 8 servings

Over time, as you make meatloaf you'll probably change a little of this, change a little of that. This is a family recipe that has been handed down through the years and become what we're sharing here. You'll find that this meatloaf slices really well. Not only does it look nice when served—it will lie beautifully on sliced bread with mayo if there's any left over.

— Dolly & Rachel

Sauce

1 cup ketchup

1 tablespoon light brown sugar

½ teaspoon prepared yellow mustard

Meatloaf

2 eggs

1 (5-ounce) can evaporated milk

¾ cup old-fashioned rolled oats

1 pound 6 ounces ground beef

10 ounces ground pork

½ medium onion, finely chopped

½ cup finely chopped green bell pepper

1 teaspoon sea salt

1 teaspoon black pepper

1 teaspoon garlic powder

½ teaspoon onion powder

1 Preheat the oven to 350°F.

2 To make the sauce, in a medium bowl, stir together the ketchup, sugar, and mustard until combined. Set aside.

3 To make the meatloaf, crack the eggs into a medium bowl, mix with a fork, and stir in the evaporated milk. In a food processor fitted with the blade attachment, pulse the oats until they are about half their original size. Transfer the oats to the egg mixture. Give it a good stir and allow it to soak for 10 to 15 minutes.

4 In a large bowl, combine the ground beef and pork, onion, bell pepper, salt, black pepper,

side note

Meatloaf is one of our absolute favorite family recipes! We love to make ours with beef and pork using the ratios provided. But you can always ask your butcher for 2 pounds of "ground beef and pork" that's already combined. It's always about two parts beef to one part pork, just like in this recipe. You can also use all beef if you prefer.

garlic powder, onion powder, and ¼ cup of the sauce. Add the soaked oat mixture. Using your hands or a wooden spoon, mix until well combined.

5 Pat the meatloaf mixture into a 9 by 5-inch meatloaf pan with the insert (or a 9 by 5-inch loaf pan if you don't have a meatloaf pan). Bake for 45 minutes. Carefully remove the meatloaf from the oven and pour the remaining sauce over the top. Return the meatloaf to the oven and bake for 15 minutes more, until the sauce forms a nice glaze. Remove from the oven and allow to rest for 10 minutes before slicing.

Whipped Potatoes

prep time: 10 minutes • cook time: 30 minutes
makes 6 to 8 servings

If you're thinking there are a lot of potato recipes in this book, you're right. They were a staple of our lives growing up, and that's never changed. They're the perfect comfort food. Potatoes lend themselves to so many meals in our homes—if you come to our homes for dinner, the odds are very good that you're going to find them on the table!

— Dolly & Rachel

4 pounds russet potatoes

1½ teaspoons salt

½ cup (1 stick) butter, room temperature, plus more for serving

5 ounces half-and-half, room temperature, plus more as needed

Salt and pepper to taste

Chopped fresh parsley, for garnish (optional)

1 Wash and scrub the potatoes. Peel and remove any blemishes. Cut and quarter all the potatoes and rinse in a colander until the water runs clear.

2 Transfer the potatoes to a large pot and cover with cold water. Add 1 teaspoon of the salt and bring to a boil over high heat. Lower the heat to medium-high and cook for 20 minutes, or until the potatoes are fork-tender.

3 Drain the potatoes in a colander, then place them in a large bowl. Using an electric hand mixer, begin to whip the potatoes on medium speed. Add the butter, half-and-half, and the remaining ½ teaspoon salt. Increase the mixer speed to high and whip until light and creamy. Add more half-and-half if you desire a creamier consistency. Finish with an additional pat of butter (about 1 tablespoon) and salt and pepper to taste. Garnish with parsley (if desired) before serving.

Southern Green Beans

prep time: 15 minutes • cook time: 1 hour 40 minutes
makes 8 servings

Green beans have always been part of our lives. We grew them, picked them, canned them, and ate them while growing up. *A lot of them.* The only thing we had more of was potatoes! We also cooked our green beans a long time. That's just the way it was done then, and the way we do it now.

- 8 slices bacon
- Olive oil, as needed
- 2 pounds fresh whole green beans
- 1 medium onion, quartered top to bottom
- 1 (32-ounce) carton chicken stock
- 1 teaspoon salt
- 1 teaspoon pepper
- 1 teaspoon garlic powder
- ½ teaspoon onion powder

1. In a large cast-iron skillet, fry the bacon over medium heat until crispy, 8 to 10 minutes. Drain it on a paper towel–lined plate until cool, then chop it. Reserve ¼ cup of the bacon grease, adding olive oil if you don't have enough to equal ¼ cup.
2. Wash the green beans and drain them in a colander. Pat them dry and trim the ends. Snap them in half to make bite-size pieces.
3. Place the green beans in a large pot. Add the bacon grease, onion, chicken stock, salt, pepper, garlic powder, and onion powder. Bring to a boil, stir, and lower the heat to medium for a gentle boil for 1 hour. Remove the lid and gently stir. Taste for seasoning. Cook for 30 minutes more without the lid to allow the liquid to reduce.
4. Transfer the green beans to a serving bowl. Top with the chopped bacon and serve.

Country Loaf Bread

prep time: 20 minutes plus 1 hour 20 minutes rising • cook time: 25 minutes
makes two 9 by 5-inch loaves

This bread is simple because you just mix it in a stand mixer with a dough hook. It's a wonderful loaf bread that also makes great sandwiches. In my home, it never lasts long because my husband will grab a slice every time he passes through the kitchen. That's why I make two loaves!

2½ cups very warm water (about 110°F)

2 tablespoons active dry yeast

¼ cup sugar

1 tablespoon sea salt

6 cups sifted all-purpose flour, plus more for dusting

1 tablespoon vegetable oil, olive oil, or shortening, plus more for greasing

1 tablespoon butter, melted, plus 1 tablespoon (optional) melted, for brushing

Cooking spray or shortening, for greasing

1. In a medium bowl, stir together the warm water, yeast, and sugar until the yeast and sugar are dissolved. Allow it to sit about 5 minutes. The yeast will be foamy or bubbly, meaning it's activated. If not, then your yeast may be bad. If this happens, discard and repeat the process with fresh yeast.

2. Add the sea salt, flour, oil, and melted butter to the bowl of a stand mixer fitted with a dough hook attachment and turn the machine to low speed. Gradually add the water-yeast mixture. Increase the mixer speed to medium and mix until the dough is smooth and pulls away from the sides of the bowl, about 2 minutes. If you still have dry ingredients in the bowl, add a tablespoon of water at a time until all the flour is well incorporated. This can also be done in a bowl with a sturdy spoon if you don't have a stand mixer.

3. Grease a medium glass bowl with oil. Release the dough from the hook and place it in the bowl. Turn the dough in the bowl, coating the entire surface with the oil. Cover with a tea towel and place in a draft-free place to rise until the dough doubles in size, about 1 hour. Preheat the oven to 375°F.

4. Punch down the dough and turn it out onto a lightly floured surface. With floured hands, fold the dough in gently on all corners. Gather the edges of the dough by using your fingertips and then lift and bring the edges toward the center. Turn the dough over and repeat. Divide the dough in half with a dough cutter or sharp knife.

5 Grease two 9 by 5-inch loaf pans with cooking spray. Place half of the dough in each of the prepared pans, gently shaping it to fit. Cover both pans with a tea towel and let rest for 20 minutes for a second rise.

6 Bake the loaves until golden brown, 20 to 25 minutes.

7 Remove the bread from the oven and turn it out onto a cooling rack. If desired, brush the tops with melted butter. Cool for 10 minutes before slicing.

Encore: Chocolate Cobbler

prep time: 15 minutes • cook time: 30 minutes
makes 6 to 8 servings

Mama always kept a box of cocoa, and just like Rachel, she'd work with it from scratch. We didn't always have a lot of money for sugar, though, so we didn't get a lot of sweets. But when we did, it was chocolate we were after. This recipe reminds Dolly of those times and is inspired by Rachel's love of both cobbler and chocolate. It's an easy dish to make, and a cobbler is something you can put together as your guests are arriving and serve hot out of the oven for dessert!

— Dolly & Rachel

Cobbler Batter

6 tablespoons (¾ stick) butter

1¼ cups self-rising flour

1 cup sugar

1 tablespoon plus 2 teaspoons unsweetened cocoa powder

½ cup whole milk

1 teaspoon vanilla extract

1½ cups boiling water

Topping

¾ cup sugar

¼ cup unsweetened cocoa powder

½ cup chopped walnuts, for garnish

Vanilla ice cream, for serving

1 Preheat the oven to 350°F. To make the batter, place the butter in an 8-inch square baking dish and place it in the oven while it preheats. When the butter has melted, remove the dish from the oven and set aside.

2 Meanwhile, prepare the topping. Stir together the sugar and cocoa powder in a small bowl and set aside.

3 In a medium bowl, combine the flour, sugar, and cocoa powder. Add the milk and vanilla and stir until smooth.

4 Pour the batter mixture over the melted butter in the baking dish. Sprinkle the sugar-cocoa on top. Gently pour the boiling water over the top, place in the oven, and bake until the cobbler is hot and gooey, 30 minutes.

5 Garnish the cobbler with the chopped walnuts and serve right away, with vanilla ice cream.

NASA
ASTRONAUT
NASA
Happy

October

Halloween ~ Boo~U Meal

Halloween—Boo-U Meal

We admit it—we're always going to be childlike enough that we look forward to Halloween as much as kids do! We laughed so much putting together this meal, thinking back on Halloweens we've shared. We always go all out, and these recipes are meant to help you do the same. Prepare them before it's time to go trick-or-treating. That way, everything is ready and waiting when you walk back in the door!

Maybe we enjoy Halloween so much because we couldn't really go trick-or-treating when we were young—every house was at least a mile away. And our mama would've had to create a dozen costumes! She'd make us masks out of scraps of cloth sometimes, though. There was always fun to be had growing up in the mountains, no matter what.

As the weather started to turn cold, Daddy would sometimes build a big bonfire in the fields below our little home. It was harvesttime, and our family was large enough that it felt like we were having our own fall festival gathered around that fire, just Mama, Daddy, and the kids. Maybe that's why fall has always been a favorite time of year for us. Or maybe we just can't get enough of seeing the children in our family enjoy Halloween because we're still kids at heart.

Witches' Brew Cider

prep time: 5 minutes plus overnight chilling
makes 8 drinks

Our sister Willadeene created this concoction for our nephew Bryan, and he named it Witches' Brew. We still make it and love it. And it's safe to have at a party with kids because you don't need different punch bowls labeled for kids and adults—the grown-ups can just add a little something to their glass to "spice it up."

—Dolly & Rachel

- 1 gallon apple cider
- 12 whole cloves
- 7 whole allspice berries
- 1 (12-ounce) can frozen orange juice concentrate
- Handful of red-hot cinnamon candies
- 1 (2-liter) bottle ginger ale, chilled
- Cinnamon sticks, for serving
- Whiskey, bourbon, or rum (optional), for serving

1. Combine the apple cider, cloves, allspice, orange juice concentrate, and cinnamon candies in one or two large pitchers. Stir with a wooden spoon until the orange juice concentrate dissolves. Cover and refrigerate overnight.
2. Using a kitchen strainer to catch the cloves and allspice, strain the mixture into a punch bowl. Discard the spices. When ready to serve, add the ginger ale.
3. For the kids, serve the punch with a cinnamon stick. For the adults, serve with a shot of whiskey, bourbon, or rum, if desired. 😉

Opening Act: Kettle Corn

prep time: 5 minutes • cook time: 18 minutes
makes 4 cups

You can't help but think of kettle corn in the fall. Mama made a version of this in her big black iron kettle, tossing dried corn kernels, sorghum, and salt into piping-hot lard. Now we make it with corn syrup and butter, of course, and it's always part of Halloween when we're together with all our nieces and nephews. There's nothing like the buttery-sweet smell of this—it can take you right back to a fair or festival just thinking about it.

2 tablespoons vegetable oil, plus more for greasing

½ cup popcorn kernels

½ cup (1 stick) butter

1½ cups packed light brown sugar

½ cup light corn syrup

¾ teaspoon salt

½ teaspoon baking soda

1 cup salted peanuts (optional)

Special Equipment

Dutch oven

Candy thermometer

1 Line a large, shallow baking pan with foil. Lightly coat the foil with oil and set aside.

2 In a large Dutch oven, add the 2 tablespoons of oil and a few corn kernels. Cover and heat over medium-high heat until one or two of the kernels pop—this is your indicator that the pan is hot. Remove the lid and quickly add the rest of the corn kernels to the pot. Cover immediately and cook, shaking the pan frequently, until the kernels start popping, about 3 minutes. Remove from the heat. Once the kernels stop popping, uncover the pot.

3 In a separate large pot, melt the butter over medium-high heat. Add the brown sugar and corn syrup and stir, bringing the mixture to a boil. Boil without stirring until the syrup registers 300°F on a candy thermometer, 8 to 10 minutes. Remove the pot from the heat. Be ready to work quickly during the next steps!

4 Using a wooden spoon or heatproof spatula, stir the salt and baking soda into the hot syrup. This will bubble—don't be surprised when it does! Be careful; you may want to wear an oven mitt. If you'd like to include peanuts, this is the time to add them to the mixture. Add the popcorn and stir to coat everything in the syrup. Immediately spread the mixture on the prepared baking pan as thinly and evenly as possible. Cool completely, then break into bite-size pieces.

October

Sloppy Dogs

prep time: 20 minutes • cook time: 30 minutes
makes 8 servings

I wanted to create a menu for Halloween that you could make in advance and keep warm while you go trick-or-treating with the kids. Something like a sloppy joe felt natural, but I also wanted hot dogs. It occurred to me that I could cook hot dogs with the sloppy joe elements—that's where the extra broth comes in. When you get home, simply put a hot dog on a bun and add the meat sauce. That's how the Sloppy Dog was born! We use an electric skillet for this, because the meat mixture can be kept on a warm setting once it's done. But the stovetop works, too!

— Rachel

1 pound 80/20 ground beef
1 teaspoon salt
1 teaspoon black pepper
½ large onion, chopped
½ large green bell pepper, chopped
¾ cup chicken broth
1 cup ketchup
1½ teaspoons Worcestershire sauce
1 teaspoon prepared yellow mustard
2 tablespoons light brown sugar
1 teaspoon chili powder
½ teaspoon garlic powder
½ teaspoon onion powder
½ teaspoon ground cumin
8 hot dogs (we like Nathan's)
8 hot dog buns

1 Let the ground beef sit out for about 20 minutes to reach room temperature. Place the meat in a large skillet and add the salt, black pepper, onion, bell pepper, and ¼ cup of the chicken broth and cook over medium-high heat, breaking up the meat with a wooden spoon until the meat is no longer pink, 7 to 9 minutes. If needed, pour off any excess fat when done.

2 Add the remaining ½ cup chicken broth, the ketchup, Worcestershire, mustard, brown sugar, chili powder, garlic powder, onion powder, and cumin and stir to combine. Gently add the hot dogs and lower the heat to medium. Cook, uncovered, for 15 to 20 minutes. If you're using an electric skillet, you can then cover it and let it rest on a warm setting until you're ready to eat.

3 Just before serving, preheat the oven to 200°F. Wrap the hot dog buns loosely with foil and warm them in the oven for 5 to 10 minutes. Place 1 hot dog in each bun, and top with some of the Sloppy Dog mixture. Serve warm.

side note Rachel is so creative. The first time she made this, I thought, "I love hot dogs, and I love sloppy joes. Why didn't I think of that?!"
—Dolly

Mac and Cheese

prep time: 20 minutes • cook time: 35 minutes
makes 6 to 8 servings

There's nothing quite like a good old bowl of mac and cheese. Neither one of us can think of anyone we know who doesn't like mac and cheese, and we certainly love it. Ours is made with a variety of cheeses, but we had to include a little Velveeta—ultimately, that's what makes this version so creamy and good.

- Butter, for greasing
- 1 teaspoon salt
- 2 cups elbow macaroni
- 1 tablespoon extra-virgin olive oil
- 2½ cups shredded cheddar cheese
- 2½ cups shredded Monterey Jack cheese
- 2 eggs, beaten
- 1 cup whole milk, room temperature
- ½ cup sour cream
- 2 tablespoons butter, melted
- 1 teaspoon mustard powder
- 1 (8-ounce) block Velveeta, cubed

1. Preheat the oven to 350°F. Grease a 9 by 13-inch baking pan with butter.
2. Place a large saucepan of water over medium heat, add the salt, and bring it to a boil. Add the macaroni and cook for 2 to 3 minutes less than indicated on the package. Don't overcook and don't rinse. Drain the macaroni well in a colander, return it to the pot, and add the olive oil. Gently stir to coat so the macaroni doesn't stick together.
3. Set aside ¼ cup of the shredded cheddar and ¼ cup of the shredded Monterey Jack for topping.
4. In a large bowl, use a wooden spoon to combine the eggs, milk, sour cream, butter, and mustard powder. Add the Velveeta, remaining cheddar and remaining Monterey Jack, stirring well. Add the macaroni to the mixture and stir until well combined and the macaroni is nicely coated.
5. Transfer the mixture to the prepared pan, spreading it evenly, and sprinkle the top with the reserved cheddar and Monterey Jack cheeses. Bake until the cheeses are bubbly, 20 to 25 minutes.
6. Remove from the oven and let rest for 15 to 20 minutes to thicken before serving.

Jack-o'-Lantern Serving Bowls with Fresh Vegetables

prep time: 15 minutes
makes 8 servings

The first time we saw this, we thought it was just the cutest thing! Bell peppers are the right size and shape to use as serving bowls—fill them with vegetable bites, or put dip in one or two of them. It's fun, simple, colorful, and creative!

— Dolly & Rachel

- 4 large bell peppers in assorted colors and shapes
- 1 medium bell pepper, cored, seeded, and cut lengthwise into ¼-inch-thick slices
- 2 large carrots, cut into sticks
- 1½ cups broccoli florets
- 1½ cups cauliflower florets

1. Cut the tops off of the large bell peppers, as you would the lid of a pumpkin. Scoop out the seeds, ribs, and center of each pepper. Carefully carve a jack-o'-lantern face in each pepper. If you prefer, use a marker to draw a face on each (but if you do, be sure the peppers are used only for serving and décor—unless you're using markers with edible ink).
2. Fill one pepper with the cut pepper slices, one with carrot sticks, one with broccoli, and one with cauliflower. Serve on a platter or wooden serving board with other assorted fresh vegetables.

Puppy Trix and Treats

prep time: 5 minutes
makes 8 servings

Simply put, this is the kids' version of Chex Mix. It's a simple combination of salty and sweet with just enough different things in it for everyone to enjoy—and it ensures every handful is as delicious as the next, no matter what you grab. Trust us—you'll see plenty of adults reaching for it, too!

— Dolly & Rachel

1 (10.5-ounce) bag Chex Mix peanut butter–chocolate Muddy Buddies (you can always substitute roughly 3 cups of your own "chow" mix made with Chex cereal for this)

1¼ cups M&M's

4 cups mini pretzels

1 (8-ounce) Snak-Saks bag Oreo Mini Chocolate Sandwich Cookies (roughly 3 cups)

⅔ cup butterscotch morsels

In a large serving bowl, combine the Muddy Buddies, M&M's, mini pretzels, Oreo Minis, and butterscotch morsels. Serve as a grab-and-go snack mix.

Brainiac Jell-O

prep time: 15 minutes plus 3 hours chilling • cook time: 5 minutes
makes 8 servings

Yes, we have a recipe that explains how to make a "brain" and "brain juice." That just shows how much fun we've had creating this Halloween menu. You will have to go to the party store for a brain-shaped gelatin mold or order one online, but they do exist! When you turn out the Jello-O—it's amazing—it really looks like a brain! Add the ooey, gooey brain juice, and watch everyone's face when they see it!

Brain

Cooking spray, for greasing

1¾ cups boiling water

2 (6-ounce) boxes peach-flavored Jell-O

1 (5-ounce) can evaporated milk

¾ cup cold water

Brain Juice

1 (3-ounce) box strawberry-flavored Jell-O

2 tablespoons cornstarch

1 cup cold water

Gummy worms and eyeballs, for garnish (optional)

Special Equipment

Brain-shaped gelatin mold

1 Wash, dry, and prep the brain mold with cooking spray.

2 To make the "brain," in a medium glass bowl, combine the boiling water and peach Jell-O mixes, stirring until thoroughly dissolved, about 2 minutes. Stir in the evaporated milk and cold water, blending thoroughly. Pour the mixture into the brain mold. Cover and refrigerate until firm, at least 3 hours.

3 To make the "brain juice," in a small glass bowl, combine the strawberry Jell-O mix and cornstarch. Stir in the cold water. Microwave on high for 1 minute, then stir again to dissolve the strawberry Jell-O and cornstarch. Allow the mixture to cool to room temperature. It will thicken some but still be pourable.

4 To serve, remove the brain mold from the refrigerator. Fill a large bowl with warm water. Dip the Jell-O mold into the water, immersing it so that the water comes just up to—but not over—the edge, for 15 seconds. Lift the mold from the water. Place a serving plate upside down over the open side of the mold. Holding the mold and the plate together, invert and shake them slightly to loosen the gelatin. Carefully pull the

continued

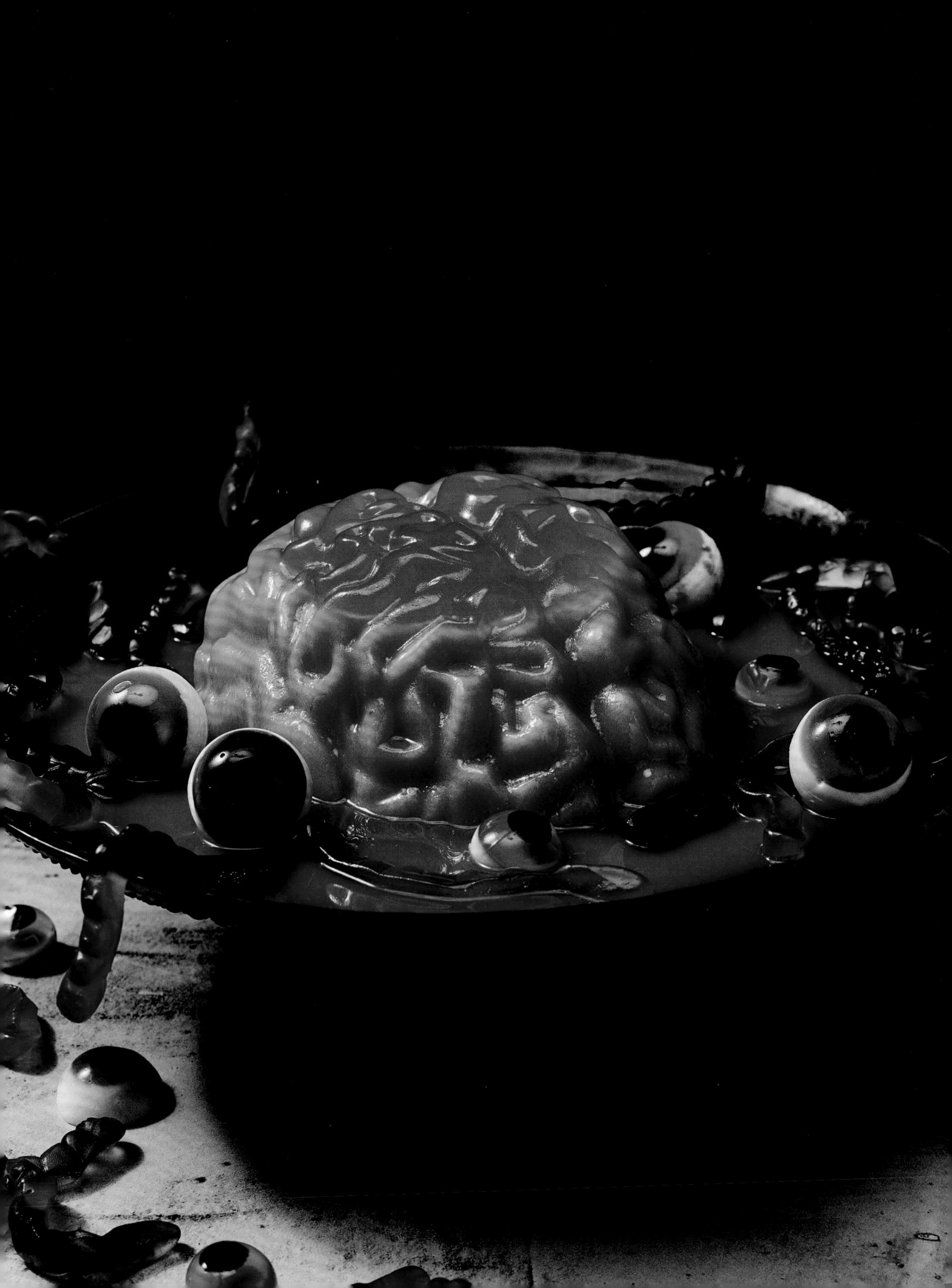

Brainiac Jell-O, continued

mold away. If necessary, repeat the warm water dip. If the gelatin has softened, put the dish into the refrigerator for a few minutes to firm up.

5 Spoon some of the strawberry brain juice around the brain on the serving plate. Spoon more brain juice over the top, garnish with gummy candy (if desired), and serve.

side note

When you're purchasing the brain mold, it's the perfect time to also grab gummy worms and eyeballs!

Encore: Spider Cake

prep time: 30 minutes • cook time: 1 hour
makes 8 servings

Halloween can be so much fun with the kids around, and it seems like they're always roaming through the kitchen. Like every aspect of our Halloween menu, this cake can be made in advance . . . and the kids can help decorate it. Add the licorice legs and the eyes—and don't forget the glaze. It's just so cute!

—Dolly & Rachel

Cake

Cooking spray, for greasing

1½ cups (3 sticks) butter, softened

2 cups granulated sugar

4 eggs

1 tablespoon vanilla extract

½ teaspoon almond extract

3 cups all-purpose flour

6 tablespoons cornstarch

2 teaspoons baking powder

1½ teaspoons salt

1 cup whole milk

Glaze

2 tablespoons butter

2½ cups powdered sugar

2 to 3 tablespoons whole milk

½ teaspoon vanilla extract

To Assemble

Black licorice (we like Twizzlers)

Orange and black sprinkles (optional)

Candy corn (optional)

1 Preheat the oven to 350°F. Grease a 12-cup Bundt cake pan with cooking spray.

2 To make the cake, in a medium bowl and using an electric hand mixer, or in a stand mixer fitted with the paddle attachment, beat the butter and sugar on medium-high speed until light and fluffy, about 2 minutes. Add the eggs, one at a time, mixing well after each is added. Add the vanilla and almond extracts and continue mixing until blended and smooth.

3 In a large bowl, whisk together the flour, cornstarch, baking powder, and salt. Add half of the dry ingredients to the wet ingredients. With the hand mixer or the stand mixer fitted with the paddle attachment, beat on medium-high speed until well combined. Pour in the milk and beat until just incorporated. Add the remaining dry ingredients and continue beating until the batter is smooth, being careful not to overmix.

continued

Spider Cake, continued

4 Pour the batter into the prepared pan and bake until golden brown and a toothpick inserted in the center comes out clean, about 55 minutes.

5 Allow the cake to rest in the pan for 10 minutes, then turn it out onto a cooling rack to cool completely. Carefully transfer the cooled Bundt cake from the rack to a cake plate.

6 To make the glaze, in a small saucepan, melt the butter over medium heat. Remove from the heat, then add the powdered sugar and 2 tablespoons of the milk. Whisk together until the powdered sugar dissolves and the glaze is smooth. If the mixture is too thick, add another tablespoon of milk—the glaze should coat the back of a spoon nicely. Add the vanilla and stir, then spoon the glaze over the cooled cake.

7 To make the "spider," insert four pieces of the licorice into each side of the cake to create legs (eight total). Cut a stick of licorice into two 1-inch-long slices and insert them for the eyes. You can also garnish the top with orange and black sprinkles, if you wish—SPOOKY!

side note

Since it's Halloween and you no doubt have some candy corn hanging around, another option is to use it for the eyes and nose (as shown in the photo, opposite)!

November

Thanksgiving—Let's All Gather

Thanksgiving—Let's All Gather

In our family, Thanksgiving always has been—and always will be—a time to stop and reflect and be thankful. There's no better reminder of how important it is to do that than seeing people together around a table filled with food.

That food does not have to be traditional, of course. But there's something about the sights and smells of turkey and gravy, cornbread dressing, potatoes, sweet potatoes, vegetables, and pumpkin pie that helps us remember what the day is all about. Well-prepared food can bring people together all year long, but this combination of tastes and aromas stirs up so many memories.

These days, it can be nice to go around the table and share what you're thankful for—we sometimes do it from oldest to youngest. Mama used to say a brief prayer, thanking God for getting us all through another year. And though we didn't have turkey and cranberries—it was more likely to be chicken on her table—the importance of the holiday was still the same.

It's funny how some things change while others never do. The recipes may be different or new, but we still gather in some way at Thanksgiving. The same scent of sage fills the kitchen; the same laughter can be heard through the house. And the meal we prepare still reminds us how fortunate we are. And how blessed.

Opening Act: Classic Spinach Artichoke Dip with Fresh Vegetables

prep time: 15 minutes • cook time: 35 minutes
makes 8 servings

The hardest part of this dish is getting all the water out of the spinach. If that's the biggest challenge, you can already tell this is going to come together with ease. It's not only made in a single pan, but the same skillet it's baked in can double as the serving dish!

— Dolly & Rachel

Cooking spray, for greasing

1 (10-ounce) package frozen spinach, thawed

½ cup mayonnaise

½ cup sour cream

1 (8-ounce) block cream cheese, room temperature

1 (12-ounce) container marinated artichoke hearts, drained and chopped

1 cup shredded mozzarella cheese

1 teaspoon salt

1 teaspoon pepper

Sourdough or French bread, sliced, for serving

Assorted raw vegetables, for serving

1 Preheat the oven to 400°F. Grease an 8-inch cast-iron skillet with cooking spray.

2 Place the thawed spinach in a colander. Drain as much water from the spinach as possible. It's helpful to place a bowl over the top of the spinach (while it's in the colander) and mash it down to press out the excess water. Roughly chop the drained spinach and set aside.

3 In a medium bowl, combine the mayonnaise, sour cream, and cream cheese, mixing until smooth. Stir in the artichoke hearts, spinach, mozzarella, salt, and pepper. Spread the mixture evenly into the prepared skillet. Cover with foil and bake until hot and bubbly, about 35 minutes.

4 This can be served in the skillet—just be sure to wrap the handle with a kitchen towel to prevent any burns. Serve with sliced bread and fresh vegetables.

Thanksgiving Turkey and Gravy

prep time: 25 minutes plus thawing and resting time
cook time: 3 hours 15 minutes
This recipe uses a 14-pound turkey, which will feed 8 to 10 people.

The keys to a perfect turkey? First, make sure the bird is properly thawed and prepped for cooking. Then insert some butter—we use herb butter—under the skin and brush more over the skin itself. And don't cook it too fast or for too long. Enjoy the aroma that fills your kitchen from the carrots, celery, onions, and apples, as well as thyme and sage. It just *is* Thanksgiving. It smells like home.

— Dolly & Rachel

Herb Butter

1 cup (2 sticks) butter, softened

1 teaspoon salt

½ teaspoon pepper

5 garlic cloves, minced

1 teaspoon chopped fresh rosemary

1 teaspoon chopped fresh thyme

1 teaspoon chopped fresh sage

Turkey

1 (14-pound) whole turkey

1 bunch celery, washed, trimmed, and halved crosswise

2 large onions, peeled and quartered

2 apples, cored and quartered

Cooking spray, for greasing

1 pound carrots, washed, trimmed, and halved crosswise

1 teaspoon salt

1 sprig thyme

A few sage leaves

Fresh parsley, for serving

Gravy

2 cups drippings from the roasting pan

Chicken stock, as needed

¼ cup cold water

2 tablespoons all-purpose flour

Pinch of salt

Special Equipment

Roasting pan

Kitchen twine

1 To make the herb butter, place the butter in a small bowl. Mash the salt, pepper, garlic, rosemary, thyme, and sage into the butter using a fork. If making well in advance, cover with plastic wrap and chill in the refrigerator until needed. You can make this the day before and bring back to room temperature before preparing the turkey.

2 To cook the turkey, move the oven rack to the bottom position and preheat the oven to 350°F.

continued

Thanksgiving Turkey and Gravy, continued

3 Remove the turkey from the refrigerator, removing all packaging, the giblets bag, and any ties around the legs. Pat the turkey dry and transfer it to a large cutting board.

4 Lift the skin and, using a spoon, gently separate it from the breast meat. Insert 1 heaping tablespoon of the herb butter under the skin on each side of the turkey breast. With a pastry brush, brush the remaining herb butter all over the rest of the skin of the turkey.

5 Into the cavity of the turkey insert 1 halved celery stalk, 2 onion quarters, and 2 apple quarters.

6 Prepare a roasting pan with cooking spray. Line the pan with the carrots and the remaining celery, onion, and apple pieces.

7 Sprinkle the turkey with the salt and tuck the wings underneath the bird. Place the thyme and a few sage leaves into the cavity of the bird (for seasoning). Tie the turkey legs with kitchen twine and let the turkey sit for 30 minutes at room temperature. Transfer the turkey to the oven and reduce the oven temperature to 325°F.

8 Cook the turkey for 1 hour 30 minutes. Then, using a turkey baster, baste the turkey with juices from the pan. Tent the turkey loosely with foil and continue cooking for 1 hour 30 minutes more. The turkey is done when a meat thermometer inserted into the thickest area of the thigh registers 160°F.

9 Remove the turkey from the oven and let it rest for 30 minutes. Transfer the turkey to a serving platter lined with parsley. Spoon the cooked vegetables from the pan into a serving bowl.

10 To make the gravy, in a medium saucepan, bring the drippings to a boil. If, for any reason, you are short on drippings from the roasting pan, supplement with chicken stock to make 2 cups.

11 In a mason jar with a lid, combine the cold water, flour, and salt. Place the lid on the jar, tighten it, and shake until the flour and water are well incorporated. You don't want any lumps of flour. Pour the contents of the jar into the boiling broth and whisk well to combine.

12 Lower the heat to medium and allow the gravy to simmer until it's thickened to your liking, 2 to 3 minutes. If it's too thick, add more drippings or stock.

13 Carve the turkey and serve with gravy.

side note The general rule of thumb for defrosting a turkey is 1 day for every 5 pounds. If you have a frozen 14-pound turkey, you'll need to thaw it in the refrigerator for 2½ to 3 days.

Sweet Potato Casserole

prep time: 15 minutes • cook time: 45 minutes
makes 8 servings

The sweet potato is a vegetable that's perfect for the fall—the color and the flavor always make us think of harvesttime. Rachel likes to cover her casserole with marshmallows. You have to—it's just one of those things. But she also adds some pecans on top—we love the taste they add, making this extra special.

— Dolly & Rachel

½ cup (1 stick) butter, room temperature, plus more for greasing

5 large sweet potatoes, peeled and quartered

½ cup packed light brown sugar

1 teaspoon vanilla extract

1 teaspoon salt

1 teaspoon ground cinnamon

½ cup chopped raw pecans

2 cups miniature marshmallows

1 Preheat the oven to 350°F. Butter a 9 by 13-inch baking pan.

2 Place the sweet potatoes in a large pot and cover with cold water. Bring to a boil over high heat, then lower the heat to maintain a low boil and cook until fork-tender, about 20 minutes.

3 Drain the potatoes in a colander and transfer them to a large bowl. Add the brown sugar, butter, vanilla, salt, and cinnamon and mash using a potato masher until well combined.

4 Transfer the mashed sweet potato mixture to the prepared baking pan, smoothing the top. Sprinkle it with the pecans, then cover the casserole evenly with the marshmallows. Cover with foil and bake for 20 minutes. Remove the foil and bake until the marshmallows are golden brown, about 5 minutes more.

5 Remove from the oven and set aside to cool for 15 minutes before serving.

Holiday Potatoes

prep time: 25 minutes • cook time: 20 minutes
makes 10 to 12 servings

When the holiday season arrives, why not dress up your mashed potatoes! That's what we do. All it takes is some cream cheese, sour cream, a little garlic, and your mixer!

—Dolly & Rachel

5 pounds russet potatoes

1½ teaspoons salt

1 teaspoon garlic paste, or 1 garlic clove, minced

8 tablespoons (1 stick) butter, room temperature

4 ounces cream cheese, room temperature

½ cup sour cream

1 cup whole milk, room temperature

2 tablespoons chopped fresh parsley, for garnish

Ground pepper to taste

1 Wash, peel, and quarter the potatoes. Place them in a colander and rinse under cold water until the water runs clear. Transfer the potatoes to a large pot. Fill with cold water to cover the potatoes by 2 inches and add 1 teaspoon of the salt. Bring to a boil, then lower the heat to medium and cook until fork-tender, about 20 minutes.

2 Drain the potatoes in a colander, then transfer them to a large bowl or the bowl of a stand mixer. Add the remaining ½ teaspoon salt, the garlic, 6 tablespoons of the butter, the cream cheese, sour cream, and ½ cup of the milk. Using an electric hand mixer, or in a stand mixer fitted with a paddle attachment, blend on medium speed. Add the remaining ½ cup milk and mix on high speed to whip the potatoes until fluffy.

3 Transfer the potatoes to a serving bowl and top with the remaining 2 tablespoons butter. Garnish with the parsley and season with pepper.

Cornbread Dressing

prep time: 25 minutes • cook time: 30 minutes
makes 8 servings

Cornbread dressing starts with cornbread, and day-old cornbread is the absolute best to use, so make some a day in advance. The same holds true for the biscuits. Lots of people make dressing in different ways, but this is what we grew up on. We can't recall a Thanksgiving without it.

—Dolly & Rachel

Cooking spray, for greasing
2 eggs, lightly beaten
⅓ cup whole milk
¾ cup (1½ sticks) butter, melted
2 cups chicken stock, plus more as needed
2 medium onions, chopped
1 cup chopped celery
1 Skillet Cornbread (page 31), left out overnight to dry
3 Buttermilk Biscuits (page 24), left out overnight to dry, or 3 pieces toasted bread
1 tablespoon dried sage
1 teaspoon poultry seasoning
1 teaspoon salt
½ teaspoon pepper

1 Preheat the oven to 400°F. Grease a 9 by 13-inch baking pan with cooking spray.

2 In a medium bowl, beat the eggs and the milk together and set aside. In a second medium bowl, stir together ¼ cup of the melted butter and the chicken stock and set aside.

3 Place a large skillet over medium-high heat and add the remaining ½ cup melted butter. Stir in the onion and celery and sauté until the onions are translucent, 4 to 5 minutes. Remove from the heat.

4 Using your hands, crumble the dry cornbread and biscuits into a large bowl, mixing them together. Stir in the sage, poultry seasoning, salt, and pepper. Add the sautéed vegetables, stirring with a wooden spoon to combine.

5 Add the egg mixture as well as the chicken stock mixture. Mix until thoroughly combined, adding more stock as needed if the dressing seems too dry. You want your dressing to be moist.

6 Transfer the dressing to the prepared baking pan, spreading it evenly and smoothing the top. Bake until golden brown and hot, about 30 minutes.

7 Remove from the oven and set aside to cool for 10 minutes before serving.

Carrots and Peas

prep time: 10 minutes • cook time: 10 minutes
makes 8 servings

Carrots and peas may be a simple dish, but they're a magical combination. At Thanksgiving, you need a few easy dishes since you have turkey, dressing, and gravy to make. This is quick, delicious, and instantly adds color to the table.

— Dolly & Rachel

10 ounces fresh carrots, peeled, trimmed, and diced

2 (10-ounce) packages frozen peas

1 tablespoon butter

1 teaspoon salt

1 In a medium saucepan, bring ½ cup water to a boil over medium-high heat. Add the carrots and cook for 2 minutes, then add the frozen peas. Turn down the heat to medium and cover the saucepan, cooking the vegetables until just tender, about 5 minutes.

2 Drain the vegetables in a colander and transfer to a serving bowl. Add the butter and salt, tossing until well combined.

Granberry Mold

prep time: 15 minutes plus 6 hours chilling • cook time: 8 minutes
makes 8 servings

We have to have cranberries with turkey, dressing, and potatoes at Thanksgiving. We love that you can make this in advance, so there's one less part of the meal to concern yourself with on the big day. Dolly calls this a "friendly side dish," and she's right—though it's sweet, it's the kind of sweet that fits the meal itself, before you ever get to dessert.

— Dolly & Rachel

Cooking spray, for greasing

3 (3-ounce) packages raspberry-flavored Jell-O

3 cups boiling water

1 (16-ounce) can whole cranberry sauce

1 (20-ounce) can crushed pineapple, undrained

1 cup finely chopped celery

½ cup finely chopped pecans

Whipped cream (store-bought or double the recipe on page 224), for serving

Celery leaves, for garnish

1 Grease a Bundt pan or large Jell-O mold with cooking spray.

2 In a large bowl, combine the Jell-O and boiling water, stirring well to completely dissolve the Jell-O. Add the cranberry sauce, stirring until melted and incorporated. Let the mixture cool for 10 minutes.

3 In a small bowl, combine the pineapple, celery, and pecans. Add them to the Jell-O mixture and stir until well combined. Pour the mixture into the Bundt pan. Cover with plastic wrap and refrigerate at least 6 hours or up to overnight.

4 When ready to serve, remove the cranberry mold from the refrigerator. Fill a large bowl with warm water. Dip the Bundt pan into the water, immersing it so that the water comes just up to—but not over—the edge for 15 seconds. Lift the mold from the water. Place a serving plate upside down over the open side of the Bundt pan. Holding the pan and the plate together, invert and shake the pan slightly to loosen the gelatin. Carefully pull the pan away. If necessary, repeat the warm water dip. If the cranberry mold has softened, put the dish into the refrigerator for a few minutes to firm up.

5 Cut the mold into 8 servings. Serve each piece with a dollop of whipped cream and garnish with a celery leaf. If you really like whipped cream—like we do—make it a "Dolly Dollop"!

Encore: Pumpkin Pie

prep time: 15 minutes • cook time: 40 minutes
makes 8 servings

In our homes, pumpkin pie is a Thanksgiving tradition, and we know we aren't alone. This pie can be made two days in advance, but it must be covered and kept refrigerated. We enjoy it any time of year, but we have to have it on our tables in November. We also can't serve it without a generous spoonful of whipped cream on top, and we know we aren't alone in that, either!

— Dolly & Rachel

Pumpkin Pie

1 (9-inch) pie crust, store-bought or homemade (see page 32)

1 cup packed light brown sugar

½ teaspoon ground cinnamon

½ teaspoon ground ginger

½ teaspoon salt

¼ teaspoon ground nutmeg

⅛ teaspoon ground cloves

1 (15-ounce) can Libby's 100% Pure Pumpkin

1 (12-ounce) can evaporated milk

3 eggs, room temperature, beaten

Whipped Cream

1 cup heavy cream

2 tablespoons powdered sugar

½ teaspoon vanilla extract

1 Preheat the oven to 375°F. To make the pie, place the rolled-out crust into a 9-inch pie plate. Crimp the edges using the prongs of a fork or your fingers. Set aside.

2 In a large bowl, whisk together the brown sugar, cinnamon, ginger, salt, nutmeg, and cloves. Add the pumpkin puree, evaporated milk, and eggs. Whisk until well combined. Pour the mixture into the pie shell.

3 Bake for 15 minutes. Lower the heat to 350°F and continue baking until the filling jiggles just slightly in the center to indicate it's done, about 25 minutes.

4 Remove the pie from the oven and place it on a cooling rack to cool completely. If made in advance and refrigerated, allow it to sit out at room temperature for 20 minutes before serving.

5 To make the whipped cream, in a large bowl and using an electric hand mixer, or in a stand mixer fitted with the whisk attachment, beat the cream, powdered sugar, and vanilla on medium speed until well combined. Increase the mixer speed to high and whip until medium peaks form, 2 to 3 minutes.

6 Serve individual slices of pie with a dollop of whipped cream on top.

December

Christmas—A Perfect Ending to a Wonderful Year

BALSAM

Christmas—A Perfect Ending to a Wonderful Year

Christmas is a celebration. It's a celebration of Christ's birth and the joy that comes with a season enhanced by music, gifts, decorations, and, of course, food. Some ornaments are hung on the tree every year, without fail. It's the same with some dishes. There's always prime rib on our table. Here it's complemented by special items like Yorkshire pudding, crème brûlée, and a special cheese ball, to create a meal worthy of this special holiday.

As we've spent time together creating this year of meals and recipes to share with you, we've realized they reflect a lifetime of family, friends, and food. That may be no more evident than at Christmas. We're reminded of Dolly dressing up as "Granny Claus" while hosting cookie nights at home, surrounded by all the children in our family as they bake and decorate. There was the Christmas Mama, Daddy, and the youngest kids came home to discover new beds in all the children's rooms, a new color TV for Daddy, and a new dining table and living room furniture for Mama, all thanks to Dolly's success and kindness. We recall Christmases before that, where Dolly and Carl couldn't afford anything more than a tiny silver tree that sat on their coffee table and a candle placed in the living room window.

We've also been reminded that all through the years—good times and hard—food and family have sustained us. They still do. We've been blessed in many ways. And that includes the opportunity this book has given us to share these recipes with you.

Opening Act: "Tree's a Crowd" Cheese Ball

prep time: 25 minutes plus 1 hour chilling
makes 10 servings

When looking for an entertaining holiday appetizer, it's hard to top this one. (Actually, it's easy to top it—you just have to decide which option you want to use!) I enjoy being creative and sharing ideas like this—it's so much fun to make!

— Rachel

We love a good cheese ball. They look so pretty—especially this one—you almost don't want to be the first person to try it, but I don't mind being that person! Invite me over—I'll do it!

— Dolly

2 (8-ounce) blocks cream cheese, room temperature

¼ cup (½ stick) butter, softened

1 cup grated cheddar cheese

1 cup grated white cheddar cheese

1 (4-ounce) jar pimentos, drained, patted dry, and chopped

1½ tablespoons Worcestershire sauce

2 garlic cloves, minced

For Decorating (to Garnish)

Sliced almonds

Chopped fresh parsley leaves

Pomegranate seeds

3 sprigs rosemary (optional)

A few 3-inch-long red bell pepper strips (optional)

Cherry tomatoes (optional)

Assorted crackers and pretzels, for serving

1 Combine the cream cheese, butter, both cheddars, the pimentos, Worcestershire, and garlic in a large bowl. Using a fork, mash the ingredients together and stir until well combined.

2 Turn the cheese mixture out onto a sheet of plastic wrap. Shape the mixture into a ball, wrap, and refrigerate for at least 1 hour.

3 Remove the cheese ball from the refrigerator, unwrap it, then turn it out onto a sheet of parchment paper.

4 Roll and mold the cheese ball into the shape of a Christmas tree. Garnish first with sliced almonds: starting at the top, insert them in a spiral shape around the cheese

continued

"Tree's a Crowd" Cheese Ball, continued

ball to resemble a garland, wrapping around the "tree" about three times. Then, using your fingers, press in the chopped parsley all around the "tree." Lastly, press the pomegranate seeds into the "tree" in a spiral pattern as you did with the almonds.

5 The "tree topper" is up to you. One option is to use rosemary sprigs and red pepper strips. Cut the top portion off 3 sprigs and stick them into the top of the "tree." Then cut a few thin 3-inch-long strips of red bell pepper, placing them like ribbon billowing down from the top of the tree. Another option is to press or cut a star out of the flesh of a red, yellow, or green bell pepper. Or simply use a single cherry tomato.

6 Serve with assorted crackers and pretzels for dipping.

Prime Rib with Au Jus and Horseradish Sauce

prep time: 1 hour plus 4 hours chilling and resting time • cook time: 3 hours
makes 8 to 10 servings

Here, herbs—especially rosemary, but also thyme—combine with butter to create a rub that enhances all the natural flavors of a quality cut of meat. I ask my butcher to cut the meat off the rib and then tie the ribs back onto the roast. Cooking it with the ribs underneath like a tray makes for a better taste, which only adds to the enjoyment of this special cut.

— [signature]

Horseradish Sauce

½ cup sour cream

¼ cup prepared horseradish

2 tablespoons mayonnaise

1 tablespoon chopped fresh chives

1 teaspoon apple cider vinegar

½ teaspoon Tabasco sauce

¼ teaspoon sugar

¼ teaspoon salt

⅛ teaspoon pepper

Prime Rib

6- to 8-pound bone-in prime rib roast (ask butcher to remove bones, then tie them back onto the roast)

½ cup (1 stick) butter, room temperature

8 garlic cloves, minced

2 teaspoons salt

2 teaspoons chopped fresh rosemary

2 teaspoons chopped fresh thyme

1 teaspoon pepper

1 large onion, quartered

Au Jus

2 cups beef stock

1½ cups red wine

1 tablespoon cornstarch

1 To make the horseradish sauce, in a medium bowl, combine the sour cream, horseradish, and mayonnaise, mixing well. Add the chives, vinegar, Tabasco, sugar, salt, and pepper and mix well. Place in an airtight container and allow to sit in the refrigerator for at least 4 hours or overnight.

2 To prepare the roast, remove the prime rib from the refrigerator 2 hours prior to cooking to allow it to come to room temperature.

3 Adjust the oven rack so that the roast will sit in the center of the oven. Preheat the oven to 450°F. Pat the roast dry with paper towels.

4 In a small bowl, mix together the butter, garlic, salt, rosemary, thyme, and pepper. Rub the herb butter on all sides of the roast.

continued

Prime Rib with Au Jus and Horseradish Sauce, continued

5 Place the roast in a 10- to 12-inch cast-iron skillet or a roasting pan, bone-side down. Surround with the onion quarters. Roast the prime rib for 20 minutes at 450°F, then decrease the heat to 325°F and continue cooking for another 2½ hours. Check the internal temperature with an instant-read thermometer. The temperature should be 120°F for medium-rare and 130°F for medium.

6 Remove the roast from the oven and transfer it to a cutting board. Tent the roast with aluminum foil and let rest for 30 minutes.

7 While the roast rests, prepare the au jus. Layer a colander inside a large bowl. Pour the drippings and onions from the skillet into the colander. Transfer the onions back into the skillet. Place the pan drippings into a grease separator, or spoon the grease from the top and discard the excess fat. Pour the remaining drippings back into the skillet with the onion.

8 Pour the beef stock and wine into a medium bowl. Add the cornstarch and whisk until well combined and no lumps remain. Add the mixture to the skillet, stirring over medium-high heat until it thickens and reduces by half.

9 When ready to serve, pour the au jus sauce through a sieve, then into a gravy boat. Cut the prime rib into ½-inch-thick slices. Serve 1 tablespoon au jus with each slice of prime rib, along with the horseradish sauce.

Au Gratin Potatoes

prep time: 25 minutes • cook time: 1 hour 10 minutes
makes 8 servings

This dish is so special—it takes a simple food like potatoes and turns them into so much more, and for a meal this festive, you want that. After layering and baking, the cheeses, butter, and seasonings are perfectly balanced in every bite. It may even taste better the next day (if there's any left over)!

— Gabe

Potatoes

¼ cup (½ stick) butter, plus 1 tablespoon, melted

2 pounds medium-to-large red-skinned potatoes

1 tablespoon extra-virgin olive oil

1 teaspoon chopped fresh parsley

1 teaspoon salt

¼ cup all-purpose flour

2 cups half-and-half

1 teaspoon ground white pepper

½ teaspoon garlic powder

½ teaspoon onion powder

½ cup grated white cheddar cheese

1 cup grated Parmesan cheese

Topping

¼ cup crushed Ritz crackers (about 13 crackers)

1 tablespoon butter, melted

1 teaspoon chopped fresh parsley

1 Preheat the oven to 350°F. Grease an 8-inch square baking dish with the 1 tablespoon melted butter.

2 Wash and peel potatoes. Slice into ¼-inch-thick rounds and transfer them to a medium pot. Fill the pot with water to cover. Stir in the olive oil, parsley, and salt. Bring to a boil, then lower the heat to medium and cook for 12 minutes. Drain in a colander.

3 In a medium saucepan, melt the remaining ¼ cup butter over medium heat. Add the flour, stir to combine, and cook for 1 minute—do not let it brown. Add the half-and-half, white pepper, garlic powder, and onion powder. Cook, stirring constantly, until the mixture just begins to thicken, 5 to 6 minutes. Add the white cheddar and stir until melted, then add the Parmesan and continue stirring until it melts into a thick sauce.

4 Layer a third of the potatoes in the prepared baking dish and top with a third of the cheese sauce. Add a second layer, using half of the remaining potatoes and top with half of the remaining cheese sauce. Repeat to create a third layer, spreading the remaining sauce over the top. Loosely cover with foil and bake for 40 minutes.

5 Remove the casserole from the oven. To make the topping, in a small bowl, combine the cracker crumbs, melted butter, and parsley. Mix together and sprinkle over the casserole. Return to the oven and bake, uncovered, until golden brown on top and bubbling, 20 minutes more. Remove from the oven and let rest 10 minutes before serving.

Green Bean Casserole

prep time: 15 minutes plus 1 hour marinating • cook time: 1 hour
makes 8 servings

Years ago, a friend of ours shared this recipe, and we've used it ever since. It's a unique take on a classic dish. It's the consommé that sets this apart, giving it a special taste and a richness that perfectly complements the sautéed mushrooms, not to mention the rest of the meal.

— Dolly & Carl

- 5 slices bacon
- 3 (14.5-ounce) cans whole green beans
- 1 (10.5-ounce) can condensed beef consommé
- 1 pint fresh button mushrooms
- ½ cup (1 stick) butter

1 Fry the bacon in a skillet over medium heat until crispy, 8 to 10 minutes. Drain on a paper towel–lined plate. Chop and set aside.

2 Drain the green beans in a colander. Transfer to a 9 by 13-inch baking dish. Add the consommé (but do not add water as directed on the can). Cover with foil and let marinate at room temperature for 1 hour.

3 Preheat the oven to 350°F. Wash, trim, and slice the mushrooms and pat them dry. Melt the butter in an 8- to 10-inch skillet over medium-high heat. Add the mushrooms and sauté until just softened, 4 to 5 minutes. Gently pour the mushrooms and butter into the dish with the green beans and consommé.

4 Bake, uncovered, for 45 minutes. Garnish with the chopped bacon and serve.

Yorkshire Pudding

prep time: 15 minutes plus several hours chilling • cook time: 20 minutes
makes 12 servings

In my travels around the world, I'll never forget the first time I had Yorkshire pudding with prime rib. I thought, "Wow. That is the best." I later told Rachel, "We've got to learn how to make this!" Once we did, I said, "If we ever write a cookbook, we have to put this in."

I love trying new recipes. This recipe isn't difficult—just make sure your baking tin is very hot. But plan accordingly. This will be one of the last things you do for your meal. The puddings are served hot right out of the oven.

- 4 eggs
- 1½ cups whole milk
- 1¼ cups all-purpose flour
- ½ teaspoon salt
- ¼ teaspoon pepper
- 4 tablespoons beef drippings, bacon drippings, or vegetable oil

---

1. In a large bowl, combine the eggs, milk, and flour and whisk until well combined. Place in an airtight container and let rest for at least 30 minutes or, for best results, overnight in the refrigerator.
2. When you're ready to bake the puddings, preheat the oven to 425°F.
3. Remove the batter from the refrigerator, add the salt and pepper, and whisk to combine. Place 1 teaspoon of the drippings or oil into each section of a 12-cup muffin pan. Place the pan in the oven until it's very hot—almost smokin' hot!
4. Remove the muffin pan from the oven and *immediately* pour the batter into each muffin well, filling them three-quarters full. Place the muffin pan back in the oven and bake until the puddings are puffed and golden, 15 to 20 minutes. Be patient! If you open the oven too early, they will collapse.
5. Remove from the oven and serve immediately with prime rib.

Encore: Crème Brûlée

prep time: 20 minutes plus 2 hours chilling time • cook time: 40 minutes
makes 8 servings

Until I actually made crème brûlée, I never thought I'd be able to do it. Once you read the ingredients and our instructions, you'll see that you can, too. If there's anything intimidating, it may be using a small handheld kitchen torch to caramelize the brown sugar on top, but even that is easier than you may imagine.

— 

---

4 cups heavy cream
1 teaspoon vanilla bean paste
7 egg yolks

¾ cup sugar
⅛ teaspoon salt
¼ cup packed light brown sugar

Special Equipment
8 (6-ounce) ramekins
2 (8-inch square) baking pans
Handheld kitchen torch

---

1 Preheat the oven to 325°F.

2 In a medium saucepan, warm the heavy cream over medium heat, stirring gently, until it begins to steam. Remove the pan from the heat, stir in the vanilla paste, and let stand for 15 minutes.

3 In a medium bowl, whisk together the egg yolks, sugar, and salt. Pour the cream into the egg mixture, stirring until well combined.

4 Prepare two 8-inch square baking pans by pouring 1 cup very hot water into each. Place four ramekins in each baking pan. Pour the custard into each ramekin up to the point of the inner rim. Carefully transfer the pans to the oven and bake until the custard edges are set but the centers jiggle slightly, 30 to 40 minutes.

5 Remove the baking pans from the oven and carefully transfer each ramekin to a wire rack to cool completely. Cover each with plastic wrap and refrigerate for at least 2 hours or up to 2 days, if made in advance.

6 To serve, evenly sprinkle 1½ teaspoons brown sugar on top of each crème brûlée. Using a kitchen torch, caramelize the sugar until browned and bubbly.

Acknowledgments

To our dear friend and assistant Devon Larson: You are amazing. It takes so much time and hard work to make sure everything is perfect for everyone. This book is everything we imagined and more, thanks to you.

To Maurice Miner: Thank you for your talent, your time, and your friendship. You have made this such a joy each and every day.

To Kelly Snowden and the Ten Speed team: What an incredibly talented team! Thank you for such an amazing project.

To Aubrie Pick: Thank you for everything. It was such a pleasure working with you and getting to meet your sweet family.

We'd also like to extend a sincere and heartfelt thank-you to every single person who helped in the creation of this project: Danny Nozell, Steve Summers, John Zarling, Dona Hennig, Lintu Holman, Cheryl Riddle, Tarryn Feldman, Riley Reed, Cody Ratliff, SJ Ashby, Andres Martinez, Ryan Musick, Derrick Hood, Rashelle Felix, Chelsea Zimmer, Ruth Blackburn, Carlos Garcia, Alma Garcia, Alma Herrera, Nayeli Estrada, Lucero Villegas, Vance Nichols, Scott Rowenczak, Kathy Jean Williams, Ric Taylor, Matthew Grant, Carol Ziegler, Karen Steinkraus, Steve and Kay George, Ashlyn Eline, Jennifer Ward, Amanda Matsui, Matt Inman, Emma Campion, Annie Marino, Terry Deal, Gabby Urena, Jane Chinn, Allison Renzulli, Brianne Sperber, Jana Branson, Jeff Kleinman, Steve Troha, Perry and Janis Schonfeld, Heidi Cunningham, Blake McDonald, Mario Fonseca, Christian Mona, Willa B Farms Animal Rescue and miniature horses Marilyn and Winnie, Bryan Seaver, SAPS, Squadron Augmented Protection Services LLC, Kyle McClain, Steve Ross, J.B. Rowland, Kelly Ridgway, Olly Rowland, Marcel Pariseau, Danelle Stoltzfus, Terry Stinson, John Varvatos, Aldo Lopez, Bennett Lawson, Grant Osum, Mason Caviness, Jeffery Moore, Matthew Moore, Patrick Baldwin, Bradley Schnabel, Lauri Patterson, Dylan Demynn, Marcus Tramel, and Josie Brown.

Rachel would also like to thank:

My sister Dolly: You are my friend to share with, my favorite cook to cook with, and the very best person to laugh and cry with. I want to thank you for sharing this cookbook with me. It has been a dream come true. I love you.

My husband, Eric George: Thank you for your love and support, for sharing my dreams with me, and for encouraging me to always take that next step. I love you today, tomorrow, and forever.

Our children, Hannah Dennison, Clay, Greg, Jeffery, and Leila George, and our grandchildren, Ginnie, Ella, and Greggy: Thank you for participating and sharing your time and love.

My little French bulldog, Bow: Thank you for never leaving my side, and for being the best food tester ever.

Maurice Miner would like to thank:

Dolly and Rachel: There's no way to express the gratitude I owe you for entrusting me to help bring your words to life in this book. It's been a joy and a privilege to hear these stories, talk through these recipes, help you share them, and make them myself.

John Zarling: I wouldn't be typing these words if you hadn't pictured me being part of this, championed me, and believed in me.

Devon Larson: Thanks for your time, diligence, and humor throughout this process.

Kelly Snowden and the Ten Speed team: I have learned so much from you and could not have brought my portion of this to fruition without your guidance.

The friends I leaned on while working on this: You listened, offered counsel, provided encouragement, and helped me maintain my focus whenever I needed it. I'm forever grateful for your enthusiasm and support.

My family: As at so many moments in my life, your support—especially that of Robert, Cheree, Jason, and that provided by my late parents—means the world.

I owe an enormous debt to *all* the amazing cooks I now realize surrounded me as I grew up. I learned more from them than I ever knew, especially my mom, my aunt, and my grandmother. They would love this book.

About the Authors

Dolly Parton is the most honored and revered female singer-songwriter of all time. She has garnered eleven Grammy Awards and more than fifty nominations, including the Lifetime Achievement Award. Achieving twenty-seven Recording Industry Association of America gold, platinum, and multiplatinum awards and certifications, she has had 26 songs reach the top of the *Billboard* country charts, a record for a female artist. In 1999, Parton was inducted as a member of the coveted Country Music Hall of Fame, and in 2022, she was inducted into the Rock & Roll Hall of Fame. To date, Parton has donated more than 200 million books to children around the world with her Imagination Library. With James Patterson, she coauthored the #1 *New York Times* bestseller *Run, Rose, Run.* She released the bestselling coffee table book *Songteller: My Life in Lyrics* in 2020, and in 2023 followed it with another bestseller titled *Behind the Seams: My Life in Rhinestones.* That same year, her album *Rockstar* debuted at #1 on six *Billboard* charts, becoming the biggest first-week sales debut of her seven-decade career. From her "Coat of Many Colors" to working "9 to 5," no dream is too big and no mountain too high for the country girl who turned the world into her stage.

Rachel Parton George is a star in her family's kitchens—her sister Dolly would be the first to say so. The youngest of twelve children born into what proved to be a musical family from East Tennessee, she followed her siblings who—like Dolly—found their ways onto concert stages far and wide. In her teens she began performing as part of her family's musical group, touring the country, and became a songwriter in her own right. Other entertainment opportunities followed, including a starring role in the TV comedy *9 to 5*, based on the movie of the same name, where for several years she reprised the role originated by her sister on the silver screen. Retiring from performing to fulfill her desire to raise a family, Rachel has become an essential member of her sister's business operations and team, serving in an executive role that supplements a variety of Dolly's various endeavors. An avid cook and self-professed collector of recipes and cookbooks, Rachel—who also enjoys decorating, entertaining, and spending time with family—makes her home in the Nashville suburb of Franklin, Tennessee.

About the Writer

Maurice Miner is a freelance media and marketing consultant and services provider based in Nashville, Tennessee. He has spent much of his country music career helping artists connect with the public and share their stories. After an award-winning start as a radio journalist, Maurice's writing brought him success working in syndicated radio, at a major record label, and with various artists and music leaders. As an interviewer, he's spent time with such varied talents as Alan Jackson, Bonnie Raitt, Carrie Underwood, Garth Brooks, Jimmy Buffett, Kenny Chesney, Miranda Lambert, Loretta Lynn, Reba McEntire, Rod Stewart, Trisha Yearwood, and Willie Nelson. He currently serves in the role of Artist and Industry Relations for Garth Brooks's Sevens Radio Network, is a Leadership Music alum, and is a member of the Country Music Association. He has served as a Belmont University adjunct instructor and is a past recipient of the annual Distinguished Alumni Award from his hometown high school in Connecticut.

Recipe Index by Course

Appetizers

Main Dishes

Salads

Sides and Vegetables

Breads

Desserts

Beverages

Index

Note: Page references in *italics* indicate photographs.

T

V

W

Y

In memory of Aubrie Pick,
who was one of the most talented and beautiful people we've ever met,
in front of or behind the camera.

Published in the United States by Ten Speed Press, an imprint of the Crown Publishing Group, a division of Penguin Random House LLC, New York.
TenSpeed.com

Ten Speed Press and the Ten Speed Press colophon are registered trademarks of Penguin Random House LLC.

Typefaces: Colophon Foundry's Apercu, Mark Simonson's Bookmania, ITC's Bookman, and Hemphill Type's Suffolk

Library of Congress Cataloging-in-Publication Data
Names: Parton, Dolly, author. | George, Rachel Parton, 1959–author. | Miner, Maurice, 1964– author. Title: Good lookin' cookin' : a year of meals - a lifetime of family, friends, and food / by Dolly Parton and Rachel Parton George with Maurice Miner ; photography by Aubrie Pick. Other titles: Good looking cooking Identifiers: LCCN 2023042713 (print) | LCCN 2023042714 (ebook) | ISBN 9781984863164 (hardcover) | ISBN 9781984863171 (ebook) Subjects: LCSH: Cooking. | LCGFT: Cookbooks. Classification: LCC TX714 .P147 2024 (print) | LCC TX714 (ebook) | DDC 641.5—dc23/eng/20231122

LC record available at https://lccn.loc.gov/2023042713
LC ebook record available at https://lccn.loc.gov/2023042714

Hardcover ISBN: 978-1-9848-6316-4
eBook ISBN: 978-1-9848-6317-1
Premium edition (signed) ISBN: 978-0-593-83697-2
Premium edition (Target) ISBN: 978-0-593-83710-8
Premium edition (Walmart) ISBN: 978-0-593-83711-5

Printed in China

Icons on endpapers and chapter openers modified from chekman, endstern, dolva, narathip, yoga, Paul Kovaloff, antto, artur80b, nadiinko, lukpedclub, salim138, and Olena Panasovska — stock.adobe.com, and NinjaStudio — shutterstock.com.

Editor: Kelly Snowden | Production editor: Terry Deal
Editorial assistant: Gabriela Ureña Matos
Designer: Annie Marino | Art director: Emma Campion
Production designer: Mari Gill
Production and prepress color manager: Jane Chinn
Photo assistants: Ryan Musick and Derrick Hood
Photo producer: SJ Ashby
Photo retoucher: Jeremy Blum
Digitech: Andres Martinez
Food stylist: Chelsea Zimmer
Food stylist assistant: Ruth Blackburn
Prop stylist: Vance Nichols
Prop stylist assistants: Scott Rowenczak, Kelly Jean Williams, Ric Taylor, and Matthew Grant
Copyeditor: Kathy Brock | Proofreaders: Rachel Markowitz and Lydia O'Brien
Indexer: Elizabeth T. Parson
Publicist: Jana Branson | Marketer: Brianne Sperber

10 9 8 7 6 5 4 3 2 1

First Edition